Art of Being Alone in God's Presence

Art of Being Alone in God's Presence

Vinu V Das

Tabor Press

ISBN 978-0-9940194-4-8

Table of Contents

Introduction

The longing to find peace in a noisy world is a universal desire—yet for many, being alone provokes discomfort or even fear. Our culture often measures self-worth by the number of relationships, followers, or social interactions we maintain, leaving little room for the sacred pause of solitude. Yet Scripture consistently reveals that it is in quiet moments, away from distractions, that God speaks most tenderly to His people. This book, *Art of Being Alone in God's Presence: A Biblical Perspective*, explores how intentional solitude can transition from an uncomfortable state of loneliness into a transformative encounter with the divine.

A central premise we'll examine is that aloneness does not equate to isolation from support, nor does it automatically produce loneliness. Rather, solitude can become a place of spiritual rejuvenation and divine intimacy. From Jesus' own habit of withdrawing to commune with His Father, to Old Testament figures like Moses and Elijah who met God in remote, desolate regions, the Bible points us toward the life-changing potential of being alone with our Creator. Instead of viewing these times as empty interludes, we learn to see them as fertile ground for prayer, reflection, and revelation.

The book unfolds in five distinct chapters, each focusing on a particular angle of spiritual solitude. First, we explore *why* being alone with God matters—a foundational understanding of solitude as a grace-filled space rather than a punishment or accident. We then confront the emotional weight of loneliness, discovering that the same God who promised never to leave nor forsake His children can transform heartache into healing through His presence. Building on this foundation, we delve into the practical steps of turning loneliness into purposeful solitude, offering guidance on cultivating consistent disciplines and habits that anchor us in God's love. Subsequently, we examine how solitary prayer, study, and meditation can empower us to serve and influence others for God's kingdom. Finally, we draw lessons from biblical figures who themselves navigated extended periods of isolation, gleaning timeless wisdom from their experiences.

Each chapter weaves together scriptural insights, real-life reflections, and actionable advice, affirming that being alone with God is neither an outdated nor a fringe notion. In fact, amidst the endless notifications and noise of modern life, rediscovering sacred solitude may prove more vital than ever. It is our hope that readers will see solitude not as a void, but as a profound invitation—one that fosters deep intimacy with God and illuminates our purpose among others. Wherever you find yourself in this journey—wrestling with feelings of abandonment, seeking a stronger prayer life, or longing to serve in a more heartfelt way—this book provides biblical encouragement and practical tools to guide you toward a richer communion with the Lord. Ultimately, may your solitary moments become the crucible where faith matures, hope is rekindled, and the sweetness of God's presence permeates every dimension of your life.

Chapter 1: Be Alone in God's Presence

Being alone in God's presence is a profound, life-transforming experience that resonates throughout Scripture. It is in these quiet moments that we are invited to draw near to our Creator, to listen for His voice, and to let His love and truth permeate our hearts. In this opening chapter, we will explore why solitude is a fundamental aspect of a vibrant Christian life. We will consider the biblical call to solitude, study the examples set by Jesus and other biblical figures, learn to distinguish between healthy aloneness and loneliness, and discover how to intentionally seek and remain in God's presence even amidst a world full of distractions. Finally, we will identify the indicators that show us we are growing closer to God as we persist in seeking Him alone.

This chapter aims to lay a strong foundation for understanding the value and necessity of solitude in the Christian journey. While the rest of the book explores additional dimensions—such as never feeling lonely in God's presence, transforming loneliness into solitude, using solitude to advance God's kingdom, and looking at biblical examples of solitary figures—here we focus specifically on the first crucial step: learning to "be alone in God's presence." Let us begin by examining how Scripture reveals God's invitation to us to step away from our daily routines, still our souls, and experience His nearness in the quiet places of our hearts.

1.1 The Biblical Call to Solitude

1.1.1 Understanding God's Invitation to Quietness

The idea of solitude is woven throughout the Bible, from the earliest narratives in Genesis to the letters in the New Testament. Often, the English word "solitude" can carry connotations of isolation or loneliness. However, when Scripture speaks about being alone with God, it points us to a sacred meeting place—a sanctuary where God reveals Himself, speaks His truth, and renews our spirits. This sacred meeting space often occurs when people willingly withdraw from their usual surroundings to spend exclusive time communing with the Lord.

In the Old Testament, God's voice is frequently heard in moments of stillness—whether on a mountaintop, in the wilderness, or in the secrecy of one's heart. In the New Testament, Jesus models this practice by consistently seeking time away from the crowds. The repeated scriptural accounts of people "retreating" to quiet places remind us that stillness is not merely an occasional luxury but a divine invitation.

Solitude is not about escaping reality or shirking responsibilities.

Rather, it is about intentionally carving out space to be attentive to God. Much like a friend who withdraws from a noisy gathering to speak heart-to-heart with another, we too step back from life's chaos to foster deeper communion with our Lord. This is the heart of what the Bible calls us to do: draw near, be still, and know that He is God (Psalm 46:10).

1.1.2 The Pattern of Jesus Seeking Solitude

One of the most compelling reasons to pursue solitude is that Jesus Himself modeled this discipline. Throughout the Gospels, we see multiple instances where Jesus withdraws from the crowds, from His own disciples, or from the busyness of ministry to spend time alone with His Father. In Matthew 14:23, after feeding the five thousand, Jesus "went up on the mountain by Himself to pray." This was not a one-time occurrence but a habit He practiced regularly.

Moreover, we read in Mark 1:35 that Jesus rose "very early in the morning, while it was still dark," to go to a deserted place and pray. The context surrounding this verse is significant. Jesus had just spent a full day healing the sick and casting out demons. Though exhausted from continuous ministry, He prioritized solitude with His Father over additional sleep or more work. This shows us that the busier His life became, the more He needed those quiet moments.

In Luke 5:15-16, after Jesus healed a leper, His fame spread, and "great multitudes came together to hear and to be healed by Him." Yet, the passage continues, "So He Himself often withdrew into the wilderness and prayed." It is striking that as the demands on Jesus increased, He responded by seeking more solitude with His Father, not less. This pattern challenges our modern culture's tendency to equate busyness with productivity, reminding us that spiritual fruitfulness is deeply connected to quiet fellowship with God.

Jesus' example shatters the misconception that solitude is counterproductive to Kingdom work. On the contrary, His greatest acts of ministry flowed from a place of intimate communion with the Father. By frequently stepping into solitude, Jesus shows us that time alone with God is not a detour from life's calling but an essential part of fulfilling it.

1.1.3 Examples of Biblical Figures Who Spent Time Alone with God

Beyond Jesus, many other biblical figures experienced transformational moments when they spent time alone with God. Each of their stories underscores the timeless principle that God often shapes, refines, and reveals vital truths to His people in the stillness of solitude.

1. **Moses on Mount Sinai**: In Exodus, Moses spends forty days and nights on Mount Sinai to receive the Law from God. This prolonged solitude was not just a passing moment but a divine appointment. Away from the Israelites and removed from daily concerns, Moses encountered God's glory in a unique way. This encounter equipped him with the commandments that would guide an entire nation. Moses' experience reminds us that God can use solitary encounters to impart guidance for both personal and communal flourishing.

2. **Elijah in the Wilderness**: The prophet Elijah, after the monumental victory over the prophets of Baal on Mount Carmel, finds himself fleeing from the wrath of Queen Jezebel. In his distress, he journeys into the wilderness. There, an angel ministers to him, providing nourishment

and comfort. Later, at Mount Horeb, Elijah experiences God's presence, not in the dramatic wind, earthquake, or fire, but in a "still, small voice" (1 Kings 19:12). Elijah's solitude teaches us that in our darkest moments, the quiet place can become a refuge where God speaks words of reassurance and direction.

3. **Jacob at the Jabbok**: In Genesis 32, Jacob wrestles with God during the night, alone by the Jabbok River. This account highlights how solitude can become a crucible for transformation. Out of this intense, personal encounter, Jacob emerges with a new name—Israel—and a renewed sense of purpose. His life is forever changed by the divine touch he receives in the solitude of night.

4. **Daniel's Prayer Habits**: While Daniel is not typically depicted in dramatic wilderness solitude, his habit of praying three times a day underscores the principle of withdrawing to be alone with God regularly. Despite living in a hostile Babylonian environment, Daniel's commitment to secluded prayer gave him extraordinary wisdom, courage, and favor before kings.

These examples reveal that solitude is neither accidental nor peripheral in the biblical narrative. God deliberately meets His people in solitude to shape their identities, guide them in critical decisions, and deepen their relationship with Him. When we choose to follow this biblical pattern, we, too, open ourselves to profound encounters with the living God.

1.2 The Difference Between Being Alone and Loneliness

1.2.1 Biblical Perspectives on Solitude

It is important to clarify that solitude in God's presence is not the same as loneliness. Loneliness often implies an emotional ache, a sense of disconnection or isolation from others that can be painful and disheartening. In contrast, biblical solitude is a deliberate, faith-filled action of stepping away from the noise of life to connect more deeply with the Lord.

In Scripture, we see that God repeatedly affirms He is with His people. For instance, Deuteronomy 31:6 reminds us that God "will never leave you nor forsake you," and Jesus promises in Matthew 28:20, "I am with you always, even to the end of the age." These verses highlight the truth that as believers, we are never truly alone. Even in moments of physical isolation, God's presence remains constant.

The Greek word for "desolate place" or "wilderness" in the New Testament often denotes a region that is uninhabited or a solitary environment. While the word might convey a sense of barrenness, it also represents an ideal space for encountering God without distractions. Such an environment, free from the bustle of society, invites reflection, prayer, and rest in God's loving arms. From a biblical perspective, solitude is thus less about "lack of company" and more about a purposeful pursuit of the One who knows us best.

1.2.2 The Spiritual Benefits of Being Alone with God

When we seek solitude with God, we position ourselves to receive several spiritual benefits that can enrich our faith journey and daily life:

1. **Renewed Perspective**: In solitude, the everyday worries that loom large can be seen from an eternal viewpoint. By

focusing on God's sovereignty, believers often find that what once felt overwhelming diminishes in the light of His majesty and grace.

2. **Deeper Intimacy with God**: Personal prayer and meditation in quietness allow for honest dialogue with the Lord. We can pour out our hearts without pretense. In response, we often sense the Holy Spirit speaking truth, conviction, or encouragement more clearly.

3. **Increased Sensitivity to God's Voice**: Just as turning down background noise helps us hear a whisper, withdrawing from worldly distractions helps us detect the gentle nudges of the Spirit. This sharpened sensitivity can guide decision-making, foster spiritual growth, and bring clarity to life's questions.

4. **Spiritual Rest**: Solitude with God provides rest for the soul. This rest is deeper than mere physical relaxation; it is the assurance that we are safe in God's hands. Jesus invites the weary to come to Him for rest (Matthew 11:28-30), and solitude is one way we accept that invitation.

5. **Authentic Self-Reflection**: Away from external pressures, we have the space to examine our hearts in the light of God's truth. Psalm 139:23-24 speaks of asking God to search us and know our hearts. Solitude becomes the opportune time for this introspection, allowing for confession, repentance, and a renewed commitment to holiness.

In short, while loneliness often leaves a person feeling forgotten or unseen, biblical solitude reaffirms that we are indeed seen, loved, and cherished by God. It is an empowering, rather than depleting, experience. Embracing this distinction helps us step into solitude not out of avoidance, but in expectation of encountering the living God.

1.3 How to Enter God's Presence in Solitude

1.3.1 Preparing Your Heart for Solitude

Effective solitude does not occur simply by being physically alone. It is a spiritual endeavor that begins with the preparation of the heart. As we approach these sacred moments, we do well to pause, settle our minds, and invite the Holy Spirit to lead us into genuine communion with the Father.

1. **Cultivate Reverence**: Recognize whose presence you are entering. Acknowledge God's holiness, love, and authority. This can be done through Scripture reading or a simple prayer that focuses your attention on God's attributes.

2. **Practice Confession and Surrender**: Before drawing near, it is wise to examine our hearts and confess any known sins. Sin clouds our perception of God's presence, but genuine repentance paves the way for clear communication. Surrendering areas of our lives that we have been holding back invites God to move freely within our hearts.

3. **Ask for the Holy Spirit's Guidance**: The Holy Spirit is our counselor and teacher. As Jesus promised in John 14:26, the Holy Spirit guides us into all truth. Begin your solitude by welcoming the Spirit to illuminate God's Word, guide your prayers, and impart spiritual understanding.

4. **Set Aside Time and Space**: While a spontaneous moment of prayer can be meaningful, purposeful solitude often

requires scheduling. Find a location conducive to quietness—a room at home, a secluded park bench, or any place that allows you to withdraw from immediate distractions. Plan enough time so that you do not feel rushed.

When you have prepared your heart in these ways, you create an environment where deep connection with the Lord can flourish. Just as a farmer tills the soil before planting seeds, preparing your heart lays the groundwork for receiving whatever God desires to reveal or accomplish in your solitude.

1.3.2 Practical Ways to Develop a Habit of Being Alone with God

Developing a habit of regular solitude is essential. Much like any spiritual discipline—prayer, fasting, Scripture reading—it takes intentionality and consistency. Below are some practical steps to help you nurture this habit:

1. **Start Small and Grow Gradually**: If you are new to spending extended periods alone with God, begin with just 10 or 15 minutes. As you become more comfortable, gradually extend the time. This approach helps you build a sustainable practice without becoming overwhelmed.

2. **Establish a Rhythmic Routine**: Identify times in your day or week that you can dedicate to solitude. Some find the early morning best, as it sets a reflective tone for the day. Others may choose late evening, after responsibilities have winded down. Consistency in timing can help your mind and heart adjust to expect these quiet encounters with the Lord.

3. **Use Scripture as a Springboard**: Bring your Bible with you into solitude. Reading a short passage—perhaps a psalm or a portion of the Gospels—can center your thoughts on God's truth. You might meditate on a verse that speaks to your current challenges or questions, letting its meaning sink into your heart.

4. **Incorporate Prayer Journaling**: Writing down your thoughts, prayers, and impressions can be an excellent way to focus during solitude. Journaling not only provides a creative outlet for self-expression but also helps you track your spiritual journey. Over time, reading past entries can reveal how God has been working in and through your life.

5. **Practice Listening Prayer**: Solitude with God is not just about presenting our requests; it also involves listening. After you pray, spend moments in silence, asking the Holy Spirit to speak. You might sense a nudge to read a certain Scripture or gain insight into a situation you face. This silent attentiveness fosters a deeper awareness of God's guidance.

6. **Eliminate or Minimize Distractions**: Turn off or mute electronic devices if possible. Let friends or family know you'll be unavailable for a set period. If background noise is an issue, consider using soothing worship instrumentals or noise-canceling headphones. The goal is to create an atmosphere of focused stillness.

7. **Respond in Obedience**: After your time alone with God, be willing to act on any revelations, instructions, or convictions you received. True transformation arises when we not only hear God's voice but also follow it.

18

Consistency is key. Like a healthy plant that needs regular watering, a relationship with God flourishes when nurtured daily. Over time, these practices will help you develop a lifestyle where solitude is as natural and life-giving as the air you breathe.

1.4 Overcoming the Distractions of the World

1.4.1 Identifying What Hinders Your Solitude

Even with the best intentions, many believers find it difficult to maintain focus during times of solitude. Modern life is filled with potential distractions—ranging from technology to our own anxious thoughts. Before we can overcome these distractions, we need to identify them clearly.

1. **Technology Overload**: Smartphones, social media, and endless notifications can easily pull our attention away from prayer or meditation. A single alert can disrupt an otherwise meaningful moment with the Lord. Being aware of your digital triggers is the first step toward managing them effectively.

2. **Mental Noise**: Often, we carry a whirlwind of thoughts into our quiet time—concerns about finances, relationships, or work responsibilities. While solitude can help us process these issues before God, allowing them to dominate our focus can rob us of the peace that comes from being fully present to Him.

3. **Emotional Baggage**: Unresolved anger, guilt, or grief can surface powerfully in solitude. While this can be a catalyst for healing, it can also divert our focus away from encountering God if we don't consciously choose to surrender these emotions to Him.

4. **External Obligations**: Constant demands from family, friends, and work can make solitude feel selfish or impossible. Guilt over "not doing enough" can sabotage your time alone with God, especially if you haven't established clear boundaries or communicated your need for solitude to loved ones.

Recognizing these hindrances allows you to address them head-on. By naming your distractions—be they technological, mental, emotional, or relational—you become better equipped to handle them proactively.

1.4.2 Strategies for Deepening Focus in God's Presence

Once distractions are identified, the next step is implementing practical strategies to deepen focus and make your solitude more fruitful:

1. **Create a Sacred Space**: Designate a specific room or corner in your home as your "prayer space." Keep this area simple, perhaps with a comfortable chair, a small table for your Bible and journal, and minimal décor. Over time, your mind will associate this space with communion with God, making it easier to slip into a posture of worship and reflection.

2. **Set Boundaries with Technology**: Turn off notifications, place your phone on "do not disturb," or leave it in another room altogether. If you're using a digital Bible, consider putting your device on airplane mode. If you must use your phone for Scripture reading, download the passages beforehand so you won't be tempted to check other apps.

3. **Practice Centering Techniques**: When mental or emotional distractions arise, gently bring your focus back to God. Some people find breath prayers helpful—short, simple phrases repeated in rhythm with breathing (e.g., "Lord, have mercy" or "Speak, Lord; I'm listening"). These help anchor the mind and remind the heart of God's constant presence.

4. **Plan Your Time**: Write down your responsibilities or to-do list before entering solitude. By doing so, you free your mind from the fear of forgetting something important. Also, decide in advance how you will spend your solitude— whether in silent prayer, Scripture meditation, or journaling—while remaining open to the Holy Spirit's leading.

5. **Welcome Holy Interruptions**: Sometimes what we view as a distraction might be the Holy Spirit guiding us to a particular thought, person, or concern. Discernment is key. If your mind consistently returns to a specific worry, it may be the Holy Spirit prompting you to pray about it directly. Offer that concern to God in prayer, then return to silence or Scripture reading.

6. **Use Physical Posture**: Kneeling, lying prostrate, or even walking in nature can help maintain alertness and cultivate reverence. Changing posture periodically can keep your body engaged and prevent drowsiness.

By applying these strategies, you not only minimize external noise but also train your inner self to remain attentive to God. Over time, you will discover that focusing on God becomes more natural, and the distractions that once loomed large recede into the background.

1.5 Signs You Are Growing in God's Presence

1.5.1 How Solitude Transforms Your Relationship with God

One of the most beautiful aspects of cultivating solitude is witnessing how it transforms your relationship with God. Spiritual growth is not measured primarily by emotion or external achievement but by an ever-deepening trust in and love for the Lord. Below are some ways you might notice that solitude is reshaping your spiritual life:

1. **Increased Desire for God's Word**: As you spend more time alone with God, you may find yourself hungering for His Word in a deeper way. Passages you've read many times may take on new significance, and you start seeking out Scripture not only for solutions to problems but for the joy of meeting God in its pages.

2. **Greater Sensitivity to the Holy Spirit**: Persistent solitude fosters spiritual sensitivity. You become more attuned to the Spirit's prompting, whether it's a nudge to pray for someone, a conviction about an attitude, or a call to step into a particular ministry opportunity. This sensitivity is a direct outcome of spending focused time listening to God.

3. **Heightened Peace Amidst Chaos**: One clear indicator of growing closeness with God is the peace that transcends circumstances. When the storms of life arise, you find it easier to return to that center of calm you experienced in

solitude. This peace is not denial of reality but a deeper awareness of God's sovereignty and presence.

4. **Authentic Prayer Life**: As solitude becomes a regular discipline, your prayers may shift from rushed lists of requests to heartfelt, two-way conversations. You begin sharing your deepest joys, fears, and desires while also making space for God to respond.

5. **Evident Fruit of the Spirit**: Galatians 5:22-23 outlines the fruit of the Spirit—love, joy, peace, patience, kindness, goodness, faithfulness, gentleness, and self-control. Over time, regular communion with God in solitude cultivates these qualities. Friends, family, and even casual acquaintances might notice a change in your demeanor.

These changes do not happen overnight. Spiritual growth is often slow and subtle, much like the gradual development of a plant over time. However, each quiet moment spent in God's presence contributes to forming Christ-like character in us. We emerge from these encounters shaped by His love and truth, ready to reflect Him in the world around us.

1.5.2 The Fruits of Spending Time Alone with Him

When we speak of the "fruits" of solitude, we are referring to the tangible outcomes that blossom when someone consistently takes time to be with the Lord. These results are not always dramatic or immediate, but they accumulate over weeks, months, and years:

1. **Clarity of Purpose**: As you regularly quiet your soul, God can clarify your life's direction and purpose. This clarity may come through a specific calling, a renewed commitment to

a certain ministry, or a deeper sense of your unique gifts and how to use them for God's glory.

2. **Inner Healing**: Solitude can become a place of spiritual, emotional, and even psychological healing. When we allow ourselves to be vulnerable before God, we open the door for Him to address the wounds, fears, and insecurities that we often keep hidden. This can lead to breakthroughs that might not occur in more crowded or hurried settings.

3. **Empowered Obedience**: Time alone with God often strengthens our resolve to follow His commandments, not out of obligation but out of love. The more we experience His goodness and faithfulness in quiet communion, the more willing we are to surrender every aspect of our lives to His lordship.

4. **Increased Discernment**: A lifestyle of solitude helps develop spiritual discernment—knowing when God is speaking versus when we are being swayed by external pressures or personal biases. Over time, you may find it easier to distinguish truth from error and to recognize God's voice amidst life's clamor.

5. **Overflowing Compassion**: Another fruit of solitude is a heart more aligned with God's heart for people. As God's love penetrates your own soul, you naturally start seeing others through His eyes. This could manifest as deeper empathy, a willingness to forgive, or a newly discovered passion for serving the marginalized.

6. **Enduring Faith**: Finally, solitude fosters a faith that endures through trials. When life's storms hit, you fall back on the quiet confidence developed in the secret place. Even if your

circumstances do not improve immediately, the security of knowing you are anchored in God's presence sustains you.

Each of these fruits underscores the central truth: solitude with God is never wasted time. It is an investment in eternity, a deliberate choice to abide in the Vine (John 15:5) so that your life can yield bountiful fruit for the glory of the Lord. The transformation may be gradual, but it is real and lasting.

Concluding Remarks

As we conclude this chapter, take a moment to reflect on your own journey with solitude. Are there routines or habits you could establish to ensure regular time alone with God? Have you identified personal distractions that you can actively minimize? Are you noticing subtle, or even profound, transformations in your relationship with the Lord as you pursue this practice? Remember, the goal of solitude is not simply to achieve a quiet mind but to draw near to the living God, who longs to reveal Himself more fully to those who seek Him earnestly.

The practice of being alone in God's presence is foundational for a healthy, growing faith. It is here, in the secret place, that we discover how deeply known and loved we are by God. It is in solitude that our spiritual lives are nurtured, our sense of calling clarified, and our souls renewed. No matter where you are on your spiritual journey—seasoned believer or someone just beginning to explore faith—there is an open invitation from the Creator of the universe to come, be still, and know His closeness. May your pursuit of solitude become a rich tapestry of divine encounters, leading you ever deeper into the heart of the One who calls you to Himself.

If you found this message encouraging, please share it with others who may benefit. God Bless.

Chapter 2: Never Be Lonely in God's Presence

Loneliness can be a daunting emotion—heavy, isolating, and at times overwhelming. In a world that prizes connection and constant social interaction, feeling lonely often brings a sense of failure or inadequacy. For believers, the complexity can increase when we wonder, "If God is always with me, why do I still feel lonely?" However, Scripture offers a comforting truth: we have a God who not only sees our loneliness but promises to meet us in it.

This chapter examines how we can reframe loneliness through a biblical lens and, ultimately, learn to rest in God's loving presence. By exploring Scripture, examining the stories of those who struggled with loneliness, and applying practical steps for focusing on God's nearness, we find that genuine, fulfilling companionship in the Lord is not a distant promise but a present reality.

2.1 Understanding Loneliness from a Biblical Perspective

Loneliness is often conflated with solitude, but they are two distinct experiences. Solitude, as discussed in this book, is a voluntary, purposeful withdrawal in which we meet God in the quiet. Loneliness, however, can strike even when we are surrounded by other people. It is an internal ache, a longing for companionship, or a sense that nobody truly understands or cares for us. While the modern world might see loneliness as something to "cure" with busyness or social media, Scripture calls us to bring our loneliness before the One who understands us best.

2.1.1 The Difference Between Loneliness and Spiritual Aloneness

At its core, loneliness is the feeling of being disconnected— emotionally, spiritually, or physically—from others. Spiritual aloneness, by contrast, can be a season or situation in which we withdraw from human interaction to focus on God, but this is not accompanied by the despair or isolation that define loneliness. To clarify:

- **Loneliness** is often characterized by despair, a sense of abandonment, or an internal question: "Does anyone care about me?"

- **Spiritual Aloneness** (or biblical solitude) is a conscious choice, made in faith and grounded in hope. We intentionally step away from daily distractions to deepen our relationship with the Lord.

27

Crucially, loneliness can afflict even the most extroverted person, while spiritual aloneness can be embraced even by someone who has a bustling family life and large community. Being physically alone does not necessarily lead to loneliness, nor does being with people always preclude it.

Yet, God is not indifferent to our feelings of loneliness. The very fact that Scripture addresses the plight of the "lonely" or those who feel forsaken indicates that God sees our emotional struggles. From the Garden of Eden, where God proclaimed "It is not good that man should be alone" (Genesis 2:18), to the promises Jesus made to remain with His disciples "always, even to the end of the age" (Matthew 28:20), God makes it clear that His design is for us to experience abiding fellowship—with Him first and foremost, and with one another in healthy ways.

2.1.2 Biblical Characters Who Struggled with Loneliness

Although we often read stories of great faith in the Bible, we also encounter moments where some of Scripture's central figures wrestled with deep loneliness. Their honest testimonies provide insight into how God responds to those who feel alone, abandoned, or misunderstood.

1. **Job's Mourning and Isolation:** After losing his children, wealth, and health in rapid succession, Job's life was plunged into darkness. His friends initially tried to comfort him, but as they attempted to assign blame, Job found himself utterly misunderstood and alone in his pain. He exclaimed: "My relatives have failed, and my close friends have forgotten me" (Job 19:14). Though he felt forsaken, God never left him. Through Job's story, we see that

profound loneliness can coexist with unshaken faith, and that God reveals Himself powerfully in our trials, often correcting our misconceptions and deepening our trust in Him.

2. **Hagar's Wilderness Experience:** After bearing Abraham's son Ishmael, Hagar was cast into the wilderness at Sarah's insistence. In Genesis 16 and 21, we find Hagar crying out in desperation, believing she and her child would die alone. Yet in these moments, God appears to Hagar, providing water and hope. She names Him "El Roi," meaning "the God who sees" (Genesis 16:13). Hagar's story comforts those who feel marginalized or invisible, reminding us that God's presence extends to those exiled—literally or metaphorically—to life's wilderness.

3. **Jeremiah's Lament:** Known as the "Weeping Prophet," Jeremiah carried a heavy burden in delivering God's warnings to a rebellious nation. His message often isolated him from the people he was called to serve. In Jeremiah 15:17, he laments that he did not sit in the company of revelers but sat alone because of God's hand upon him. Though he felt isolated, the Lord reassured him, promising to make him a fortified bronze wall against adversaries (Jeremiah 15:20). Jeremiah's experience highlights how loneliness can be part of a calling that demands faithfulness in the face of widespread opposition or misunderstanding.

4. **David in His Psalms:** Although David's life was full of victories, seasons of deep loneliness are scattered throughout the Psalms. He was pursued by King Saul, betrayed by close allies, and misunderstood by his own family. In Psalm 25:16, David cries, "Turn Yourself to me,

and have mercy on me, for I am desolate and afflicted." Yet, throughout his lamentations, David almost always concludes with a declaration of trust in God's unfailing love. His example shows that honest expressions of loneliness need not be sanitized but can lead us into deeper reliance on God.

5. **Paul's Imprisonment and Desertion:** In the New Testament, the Apostle Paul faced loneliness during his imprisonment. Writing to Timothy, he shares how in his first defense, "no one stood with me, but all forsook me" (2 Timothy 4:16). Despite the pain of feeling abandoned, Paul recognized that "the Lord stood with me and strengthened me" (2 Timothy 4:17). His conviction that God's presence overshadowed every earthly desertion underscores a key principle: even when human support fails, divine support remains steadfast.

These biblical accounts offer an assurance that loneliness is neither shameful nor indicative of weak faith. Rather, it is a universal human experience. The good news is that God consistently shows compassion toward His lonely children, drawing near and providing grace in times of isolation. By reflecting on these stories, we are encouraged to trust that God sees our private struggles just as clearly and responds with the same tenderness and power.

2.2 Finding Comfort in God's Presence

When loneliness strikes, our first inclination might be to reach for quick fixes—sending more text messages, scrolling through social media, or filling the silence with noise. However, these attempts can exacerbate the emptiness within, providing only temporary distractions. Scripture offers a more enduring remedy: finding true comfort in the presence of the One who fully understands our hearts.

2.2.1 Scriptures that Encourage the Lonely

God's Word is replete with verses that directly speak to feelings of isolation, fear, and abandonment. As you seek comfort in His presence, consider meditating on the following passages:

1. **Psalm 27:10**: "When my father and my mother forsake me, then the Lord will take care of me."

    o   This verse assures us that even the most intimate human relationships can fail, but God's care remains unshakeable.

2. **Isaiah 41:10**: "Fear not, for I am with you; be not dismayed, for I am your God. I will strengthen you, yes, I will help you."

    o   The Lord's presence addresses our insecurities. He promises both strength and practical help for those who call upon Him.

3. **Deuteronomy 31:8**: "And the Lord, He is the One who goes before you. He will be with you, He will not leave you nor forsake you."

    o   These words, originally spoken to encourage Joshua, remain relevant. They remind us that God precedes us into every unknown, guaranteeing His continual guidance and companionship.

4. **Psalm 34:18**: "The Lord is near to those who have a broken heart, and saves such as have a contrite spirit."

- Feeling lonely often coincides with a sense of brokenness. This verse highlights that God actively draws near to hearts that are overwhelmed or in sorrow.

5. **Matthew 11:28**: "Come to Me, all you who labor and are heavy laden, and I will give you rest."

    - Jesus extends a personal invitation to the weary and burdened. Loneliness can feel like an immense weight, yet Christ invites us to exchange that heaviness for the rest He provides.

Meditating on these verses can serve as a spiritual balm. Rather than filling the void with superficial comforts, immersing yourself in God's promises transforms loneliness into an occasion for deeper communion with Him. For added impact, you might memorize these passages or post them around your home as reminders of God's unwavering nearness.

2.2.2 How God Meets Us in Our Loneliness

We often think of God's presence as a feeling—an overwhelming peace or joy. While He can and does manifest Himself in emotionally tangible ways, our belief in His presence must not rely solely on our changing emotions. In seasons of loneliness, we may not always "feel" God near. Yet Scripture and the testimony of countless believers remind us that God's faithfulness is constant, irrespective of our perceptions.

1. **His Presence Brings Consolation:** In times of deep loneliness, God's presence can console us in ways human companionship cannot. This is not to diminish the importance of friends, family, or fellow believers but to

32

acknowledge that the comfort God provides reaches the hidden corners of our hearts, addressing needs we might struggle to articulate.

2. **He Offers Understanding:** Human misunderstandings often fuel loneliness. We may feel that no one "gets" us fully. However, Psalm 139 reminds us that God intimately knows our thoughts, words, and unspoken longings before they even form. When we bring our loneliness to Him, we engage with the one Being who truly comprehends our innermost self.

3. **He Reorients Our Perspective:** When loneliness becomes consuming, our world can shrink to the size of our own pain. In His presence, God gently lifts our gaze from our situation to His eternal purposes. This reorientation doesn't always eliminate loneliness instantly, but it reframes it within a broader, hope-filled context.

4. **He Invites Vulnerability:** Feelings of loneliness often arise when we fear judgment or rejection, leading us to hide our struggles. God's presence, by contrast, invites and rewards honesty. We can lay our fears, doubts, and wounds at His feet, unafraid of condemnation. In doing so, we allow His love to penetrate the very places we've guarded most fiercely.

5. **He Prepares Us for Community:** Ironically, encountering God in our loneliness can prepare us to return to the human community in healthier ways. When our sense of worth and acceptance is anchored in Him, we become less likely to cling anxiously to relationships or to seek others' approval.

Instead, we learn to give and receive love more freely, fortified by our security in God.

Finding comfort in God's presence thus involves both a shift in perspective (from self to the One who sees us) and a choice to believe in His promises above our fluctuating emotions. Loneliness, then, becomes not a dead-end but a doorway to deeper intimacy with the divine Lover of our souls.

2.3 Shifting Focus: From Loneliness to Divine Intimacy

Loneliness often results from an internal focus: we ruminate on our pain, question our value, or dwell on unmet relational needs. While acknowledging these feelings is important, dwelling on them perpetually can entrench us in isolation. Scripture points to a transformative alternative: turning our focus onto God and entering the realm of divine intimacy. Rather than ignoring the reality of loneliness, we allow it to become a catalyst that propels us toward the One whose love surpasses human limitations.

2.3.1 How Worship and Prayer Combat Loneliness

Worship and prayer anchor us in God's truth, especially when loneliness threatens to overwhelm us. These spiritual practices recalibrate our hearts and minds, reminding us of who God is and who we are in Him.

1. **Worship Shifts Our Gaze:** In moments of praise—whether through singing, listening to worship music, or speaking words of adoration—we focus on God's character: His holiness, mercy, and sovereignty. This shift from introspection to adoration can profoundly change how we experience loneliness. Rather than amplifying our

emptiness, worship magnifies God's fullness. The Psalms exemplify this pattern. Many begin with lamentation but pivot toward praise, culminating in declarations of God's steadfast love and faithfulness.

2. **Prayer Fosters Intimacy:** Prayer is not merely reciting petitions or following a ritual; it is deep communion with God. In prayer, we share our loneliness honestly—our disappointments, fears, and desires—trusting that He listens attentively. As we persist in prayer, the Holy Spirit often ministers to our hearts, providing comfort and reassurance that no human words can match. Furthermore, prayer can include listening, where we quiet our hearts and allow God to speak through Scripture, impressions, or gentle nudges of the Spirit.

3. **Thanksgiving Counters Isolation:** When we intentionally give thanks—even for small blessings—we position ourselves to see God's goodness in every situation. Gratitude draws our attention to the ways God has already been faithful. This practice can help dismantle the lie that we are utterly forsaken. Instead, we recall past evidence of His love, building confidence that He is still at work, even when we feel alone.

4. **Community of Worshipers:** While we can and should worship privately, corporate worship—joining others at church or in small groups—further combats loneliness by placing us in the context of a faith community. Even if we do not personally know everyone in the congregation, the collective act of worship testifies that we are part of something bigger than ourselves. Still, it is crucial to remember that worship is first a vertical act (toward God),

which in turn impacts our horizontal relationships (with others).

Integrating worship and prayer into daily life thus serves as a potent weapon against loneliness. These disciplines draw us into God's presence, where our emptiness meets His abundance, and our isolation finds solace in His unwavering companionship.

2.3.2 Replacing Feelings of Isolation with God's Promises

Loneliness can be perpetuated by believing lies about ourselves and about God—"I am unloved," "No one cares," or "God is far away." Countering these lies with scriptural truth is a powerful way to shift from loneliness to divine intimacy.

1. **Identify the Lies:** Begin by pinpointing the messages fueling your sense of isolation. Are you convinced that your worth depends on someone's approval? Do you believe your past disqualifies you from God's closeness? Recognizing these falsehoods paves the way for transformation.

2. **Speak God's Promises Aloud:** Scripture is replete with promises about God's love, His willingness to forgive, and His constant presence. Reading or reciting these verses can replace negative mental tapes with life-giving truth. For example, if you struggle with feeling unloved, meditate on Jeremiah 31:3 ("I have loved you with an everlasting love") or Romans 8:38-39 (nothing can separate us from God's love).

3. **Memorize and Meditate:** As you identify key promises, commit them to memory. Meditation—focusing on a verse, pondering its meaning, and personalizing its message—

36

reprograms your thought life over time. When lies resurface, the Holy Spirit can bring those stored truths to mind, reinforcing your identity in Christ.

4. **Personalize Prayers:** Transform promises into personalized prayers. For instance, you might take Isaiah 43:1 ("I have called you by name; you are Mine.") and pray, "Lord, thank You for calling me by name. I belong to You. Whenever I feel alone, help me remember that I am Yours." Such prayers deepen our bond with God, bridging head knowledge with heartfelt conviction.

5. **Celebrate Incremental Victories:** Overcoming loneliness is often a process rather than a one-time event. Celebrate small breakthroughs: moments when you sense God's closeness, find new joy in prayer, or experience peace in a situation that once triggered deep isolation. These milestones affirm that God is transforming your inner life, one step at a time.

By grounding ourselves in God's promises, we learn to interpret loneliness not as a fixed state but as an opportunity to encounter His sustaining grace. The feelings may still come and go, but they lose their power to define us because our identity is anchored in the One who calls us His own.

2.4 Practicing the Presence of God

Once we recognize that loneliness can be converted into an invitation to deeper fellowship with the Lord, we face a pivotal question: How do we sustain this awareness of God's presence beyond structured worship services or short devotional times? The secret, as saints through the ages have discovered, lies in developing a lifestyle of "practicing the presence of God." This phrase, popularized by Brother Lawrence in the 17th century, in his letters "The Practice of the Presence of God", underscores the reality that God is always near—we merely need to attune ourselves to His abiding nearness.

2.4.1 Cultivating an Awareness of God in Everyday Life

Spiritual life is not confined to church buildings or formal prayer closets. If our faith only thrives in explicitly "religious" contexts, we miss the vast majority of moments where God desires to meet us. Cultivating constant awareness involves:

1. **Mindful Transitions:** Throughout the day, we move from task to task—waking up, preparing meals, commuting to work, attending meetings, and so on. These transitions can become micro-opportunities to realign our hearts with God. A simple, silent prayer of "Lord, guide me" before starting a new task can anchor our minds in His presence.

2. **Sacred Mundanity:** Even chores like washing dishes or folding laundry can become acts of worship when done with a heart inclined toward God. Rather than viewing these tasks as drudgery, invite God into them. Reflect on the gift of a home, a family, or the resources you have, offering thanks to God as you work. This approach transforms ordinary routines into spiritual exercises.

3. **Lingering in Nature:** Psalm 19:1 declares that "the heavens declare the glory of God." Taking time to notice beauty in creation—sunrises, blooms of flowers, or the intricacy of a single leaf—can foster a tangible sense of God's nearness. Whether you live in a bustling city or a rural area, glimpses of God's handiwork are there if you look for them. Pausing

to appreciate them can recalibrate your focus and invite adoration.

4. **Scriptural Meditation:** While formal Bible study is crucial, brief Scripture meditations throughout the day help keep our minds on truth. You could choose a "verse of the day" and revisit it in moments of waiting or pause. By mulling over a single verse, you allow its meaning to permeate your consciousness.

5. **Holy Reminders:** Some believers find it helpful to set alarms on their phones or place sticky notes in key locations to remind themselves to pause and acknowledge God's presence. These reminders are not empty rituals but prompts for genuine engagement with Him.

Through these habits, we slowly train ourselves to perceive God's involvement in every dimension of life. This shift can significantly reduce feelings of loneliness, as we become more aware that the One who created the universe consistently desires fellowship with us, whether we are in a church pew or behind a desk at work.

2.4.2 Living with the Assurance That God Is Always Near

Even if we intellectually assent that "God is everywhere," truly living with that assurance can be challenging. Doubts, disappointments, and daily stresses can obscure our spiritual vision. Yet Scripture urges us to stand firm on the reality of God's omnipresence and loving commitment to His children:

1. **God's Omnipresence:** Psalm 139:7-10 famously states that there is no place we can flee from God's Spirit. Whether we ascend to the heavens or make our bed in the depths, He is

there. This truth is a bedrock foundation: we cannot outrun God's presence, nor can we ever "lose" Him.

2. **The Indwelling Holy Spirit:** In the New Testament, believers receive the Holy Spirit who dwells within us (1 Corinthians 6:19). This remarkable truth surpasses the idea that God is simply near us; He is literally at work within us, guiding, comforting, and sanctifying us. Reminding ourselves that our very bodies are temples of God's Spirit can combat the sense of disconnection that loneliness often engenders.

3. **Communion in Christ:** Jesus referred to Himself as the vine and believers as the branches (John 15:5). This analogy portrays an unbreakable, life-giving union—Christ's own life flows into us. Such imagery is more intimate than a friend walking beside us; it's God's own life animating ours. We remain "in Christ," and He remains in us.

4. **Spiritual Discernment:** Discerning God's presence may involve recognizing subtle promptings or "coincidences" that demonstrate His involvement. Over time, patterns emerge that affirm God's closeness—an unexpected word from a friend that answers a prayer, a sudden reminder of a verse at just the right moment, or a deep inner peace in the midst of turmoil.

5. **Confidence in Trials:** The assurance of God's nearness does not guarantee a trouble-free life, but it offers profound comfort in adversity. When trials come—whether they involve health issues, relational conflicts, or financial fears—the knowledge that God is present transforms despair into hope. We can echo the confidence of Psalm

23:4: "Though I walk through the valley of the shadow of death, I will fear no evil; for You are with me."

By actively reminding ourselves of these biblical truths, we cultivate a mindset that consistently recognizes God's closeness. As loneliness arises, we can lean on the reality of His nearness, secure in the knowledge that He walks with us through every moment of our existence.

2.5 Overcoming Fear and Anxiety in Loneliness

Loneliness often pairs with fear and anxiety, especially if past hurts or disappointments have shaped a belief that isolation equals danger or rejection. For some, loneliness can intensify anxious thoughts, causing them to avoid quiet moments with God. Yet this chapter's central message holds firm: God's presence is the antidote, not the cause, of our loneliness and fears. Learning to entrust our worries to Him is both a biblical command and a practical step toward freedom.

2.5.1 Trusting God When You Feel Alone

Trust is not an abstract concept; it is built through repeated experiences of God's faithfulness. When loneliness resurfaces, we might feel tempted to question God's goodness or doubt His concern. However, Scripture is filled with directives and examples that urge us to cling to Him precisely when we feel most abandoned.

1. **Recall God's Past Faithfulness:** In moments of anxiety, it helps to remember specific instances when God intervened in your life. Perhaps He provided for you financially at just the right time, healed a broken relationship, or brought

41

comfort in grief. Listing these instances and thanking God for them can reinforce your trust in His present help.

2. **Anchor in God's Character:** Trust flourishes when we reflect on who God is: loving, holy, sovereign, and unchanging. In Malachi 3:6, God says, "For I am the Lord, I do not change." Our circumstances may shift, and friends may come and go, but God's character stands firm. Meditating on His constancy can alleviate fears rooted in unpredictability.

3. **Open, Honest Prayers:** In lonely seasons, prayers can become a lifeline. Rather than offering neatly packaged phrases, pour out your heart to God as you would to a trusted friend. Share your doubts, fears, and hopes. The Psalms model this kind of raw, honest prayer that transitions from lament to adoration, from fear to confidence.

4. **Community Support:** While the focus here is on never being lonely in God's presence, that does not negate the role of a healthy Christian community. Sharing your struggles with a close friend, counselor, or pastor can help dispel the shame often associated with loneliness. God uses the body of Christ to extend His comfort. Trusting God can include trusting the spiritual support system He provides.

5. **Surrendering Outcomes:** Trust also entails relinquishing control over how God should act or when He should act. Isaiah 55:9 reminds us that His ways and thoughts are higher than ours. This does not mean God is indifferent to our timetable; rather, He orchestrates events with divine

wisdom. Relinquishing the need to orchestrate or predict outcomes can alleviate a significant portion of anxiety and free us to rest in His sovereignty.

By embracing these practices, we dismantle the notion that loneliness must equate to despair. Instead, the very absence of human comfort becomes an invitation to experience a divine comfort that transcends our limitations.

2.5.2 How to Lean on God's Word for Strength

God's Word is both our guide and our solace in seasons of loneliness. When anxious thoughts swirl, Scripture acts as an anchor for our emotions and a lamp for our path (Psalm 119:105). Leaning on His Word involves more than cursory reading; it's an active process of engaging with the text until its truths shape our internal narrative.

1. **Daily Nourishment:** Anxiety often stems from imagining future scenarios or replaying past regrets. Immersing ourselves in Scripture each day helps us refocus on eternal realities. Even brief readings can recalibrate our minds, reminding us of God's sovereignty, love, and promises. Consistency in devotional habits builds a protective reservoir of truth to draw upon when loneliness and anxiety strike unexpectedly.

2. **Personal Application:** Select passages that resonate with your current emotional struggle—be it fear, sadness, or self-doubt—and ask the Holy Spirit to illuminate them for your situation. For instance, if you feel anxious about the future, consider passages like Philippians 4:6-7 or Matthew 6:25-34. Reflect on how these promises specifically apply

to your life, jotting down insights or even rewriting verses in your own words as a personal declaration of faith.

3. **Speak Scripture Aloud:** The spoken word has power. When fear or loneliness intensifies, verbally proclaiming Scripture can serve as a potent corrective to the negative internal dialogue. Hearing the truth of God's Word in your own voice fosters an atmosphere of faith and fortifies your heart against discouragement.

4. **Scripture Memorization:** Storing God's Word in your mind allows you to access His promises anytime, anywhere. By memorizing key verses related to trust, fear, or identity in Christ, you equip yourself with immediate spiritual resources. Such memorization is particularly helpful when external Bibles or digital devices are not readily accessible.

5. **Group Bible Study:** While personal study is crucial, group studies can broaden your understanding as others share insights and testimonies. Discussing Scripture in communities can also alleviate loneliness by fostering meaningful connections with fellow believers who are journeying through life's challenges as well.

In essence, God's Word acts as a fortress for our minds. Leaning on it means we actively use it to confront anxiety, replace lies with truth, and reinforce our spiritual foundation. When loneliness or fear strikes, we stand on the immovable rock of Scripture, finding that God's promises are indeed "yes" and "amen" (2 Corinthians 1:20).

Concluding Remarks

As you reflect on the content of this chapter, consider the following questions for personal or group discussion:

- **What are some common lies or misconceptions that feed your sense of loneliness?**

- **Which biblical promises most directly speak to your moments of isolation or fear?**

- **In what practical ways can you incorporate worship, prayer, and scriptural meditation into your daily routines to maintain awareness of God's presence?**

- **How might God be using this season of loneliness to deepen your relationship with Him or prepare you for new forms of service and community?**

Ultimately, the message here is not that you will never again feel lonely—feelings ebb and flow—but that in Christ, you need never remain lonely. Jesus Himself promised His followers, "I will not leave you orphans; I will come to you" (John 14:18). The Holy Spirit's indwelling presence confirms we are fully known, fully loved, and fully accompanied. Such awareness transforms lonely nights into sacred vigils and solitary moments into divine appointments. May you, too, discover that the One who fashioned your heart stands ready to fill it with His gracious companionship, ensuring that no believer ever truly walks alone.

If you found this message encouraging, please share it with others who may benefit. God Bless.

Chapter 3: Turning Your Loneliness into Solitude

Loneliness is a common human experience, but in the biblical journey, it need not remain a point of despair. Instead, loneliness can serve as a catalyst that draws us closer to God, transforming barren internal landscapes into fertile ground for spiritual growth. This chapter explores how to intentionally convert feelings of loneliness into purposeful solitude—an environment ripe for encountering God. While loneliness often conjures images of isolation, emptiness, and longing, biblical solitude offers an alternative vision: a sacred space where God meets us, molds us, and strengthens us for life's challenges.

In the previous chapters, we examined the nature of solitude and the assurance that we are never truly alone if we rest in God's presence. Here, we dig deeper into the process of taking loneliness itself—a raw, sometimes painful reality—and turning it into a gift of renewed fellowship with the Lord.

3.1 The Gift of Solitude

3.1.1 Recognizing the Inherent Value of Solitude

Far from being a mere remedy for loneliness, solitude emerges in Scripture as a life-giving gift. The New Testament depicts solitude as a divine invitation: the quiet place becomes the arena where God speaks, heals, and draws near to those who seek Him earnestly. While loneliness can feel like a burden, solitude is, in contrast, a precious space that fosters undistracted communion.

In Lamentations 3:25–28, the prophet Jeremiah declares, "The LORD is good to those who wait for Him, to the soul who seeks Him. It is good that one should hope and wait quietly for the salvation of the LORD. ... Let him sit alone and keep silent, because God has laid it on him." This passage acknowledges both the reality of hardship and the profound goodness found in waiting quietly before God. Notice that solitude here is not presented as punishment but as a context for growing closer to the Lord.

Similarly, Isaiah 30:15 affirms that "in quietness and in trust shall be your strength." The quietness referenced in this verse offers more than just relief from outer noise; it signals a spiritual posture of dependence on God. When we shift from a frantic search for human solutions to a restful expectation of divine intervention, loneliness begins to lose its sting, giving way to trust.

3.1.2 From Barren Emptiness to Sacred Encounter

Loneliness often feels like a desert—a place of desolation and unmet desires. But consider how God repeatedly uses desert imagery throughout Scripture to highlight the potential for encounter and renewal. When Israel wandered in the wilderness, they experienced God's miraculous provision. When Elijah escaped to Horeb, he heard the still, small voice of the Lord in solitude. Time and again, the desert, with all its stark loneliness, becomes a stage for divine revelation.

In a similar vein, our internal sense of emptiness can become the "desert" where God's presence is revealed with new clarity. In Hosea 2:14, the Lord says, "Therefore, behold, I will allure her, will bring her into the wilderness, and speak comfort to her." While originally referring to Israel, the principle extends to every believer: God can draw us into places of isolation or simplicity to speak words of comfort and transformation. The desert, or the lonely place, can thus become a meeting place for divine intimacy.

3.1.3 Loneliness as an Invitation, Not a Sentence

Viewing loneliness as an invitation aligns with the Christian understanding that God wastes no circumstance in shaping us. Zephaniah 3:17 proclaims that the Lord rejoices over His people with singing; He quiets them with His love. When our social circles fail to meet our emotional needs, or when we feel overlooked by those around us, we have an opportunity to encounter the God who sings over us in love. What appears as an unwanted condition—loneliness—can actually be a summons into deeper relationship with the One who never leaves or forsakes us.

This perspective does not trivialize the pain of loneliness. Instead, it reframes it through a biblical lens, reminding us that pain is often the seedbed for spiritual breakthroughs. Jesus Himself, in His most trying moments, retreated alone: to pray in Gethsemane (Mark 14:32–36), to prepare for His public ministry (Mark 1:35), and to align His will with the Father's in moments of decision (Luke 6:12). Each of these instances underscores that solitude is not a last resort but a strategic posture for encountering the divine.

3.2 Embracing Solitude as a Spiritual Discipline

3.2.1 From Occasional Relief to Lifelong Rhythm

Many Christians see solitude as a temporary measure—something to seek during crises or at spiritual retreats. While such moments of retreat are beneficial, the biblical invitation goes further, calling us to make solitude a habitual practice, embedded in the rhythms of daily life. In the same way that prayer, fasting, and Bible study are recognized spiritual disciplines, solitude too deserves a consistent place in our devotional routines.

1 Timothy 4:7–8 exhorts believers to "exercise yourself toward godliness. For bodily exercise profits a little, but godliness is profitable for all things." Though solitude is not mentioned explicitly, the principle of spiritual "exercise" implies training, repetition, and intentional effort. By incorporating solitude into our routines—perhaps setting aside a short block of time each morning or evening—we cultivate a resilience that can only be gained through consistent practice.

3.2.2 Practical Guidelines for Engaging in Solitude

1. **Identify Your Spaces**: Whether it's a quiet room at home, a secluded corner of a local park, or even your car in a calm parking lot, designate a space conducive to reflection. The

goal is to minimize distractions so that your mind is free to focus on God without constant interruption.

2. **Begin with Stillness**: At the start of each solitude session, take a few moments to settle your spirit. Reflect on Psalm 62:5, "My soul, wait silently for God alone, for my expectation is from Him." This waiting is both a physical and mental pause that allows you to shift from life's busyness into God's presence.

3. **Incorporate Silent Prayer**: While spoken prayer or journaling can be rich, consider including periods of silence. In that silence, invite the Holy Spirit to search your heart. Resist the urge to fill the emptiness with words. Let God speak, even if you don't hear an immediate response. This teaches trust and patience in the divine timetable.

4. **Combine with Scripture Meditation**: Read a short biblical passage slowly, perhaps multiple times, pausing to reflect on a single verse or phrase. In 2 Chronicles 7:14, we are reminded that if God's people "humble themselves, and pray and seek My face," the Lord will respond. As you meditate on Scripture, let it serve as a mirror that reveals your heart, as well as a window that provides a glimpse into God's.

5. **End with Thanksgiving**: Before concluding your solitude, spend a few moments in thanksgiving. Thank God for insights gained, for His constant love, and for any peace or clarity He has granted. By finishing with gratitude, you cultivate an attitude of reliance and hope, anchoring the session in worship rather than self-focus.

3.2.3 Solitude Versus Isolation: A Crucial Distinction

One of the pitfalls for those who seek solitude—especially when struggling with loneliness—is confusing constructive solitude with self-imposed isolation. Proverbs 18:1 warns, "A man who isolates himself seeks his own desire; he rages against all wise judgment." Isolation can lead to spiritual stagnation and an echo chamber of negative thoughts, whereas true biblical solitude fosters openness to God's correction, love, and guidance.

- **Isolation** closes the door to constructive feedback, risking entrapment in self-deception.

- **Solitude** keeps communication lines with God open, inviting correction and affirmation from Him.

This distinction ensures that our pursuit of solitude remains a healthy, life-giving exercise rather than a retreat from accountability or community. Embracing solitude as a discipline allows us to balance time alone with God and engagement with fellow believers, cultivating a heart that is both intimately connected with the Lord and responsibly present in the body of Christ.

3.3 Spiritual Growth Through Solitude

3.3.1 Encountering God's Transformative Presence

Biblical solitude is not merely about clearing distractions; it is a crucible for spiritual refinement. When believers consistently enter solitude, they create fertile ground for God's transformative work. In 2 Corinthians 3:18, Paul writes, "But we all, with unveiled face, beholding as in a mirror the glory of the Lord, are being transformed into the same image from glory to glory." While this transformation can occur in various contexts, solitude uniquely positions us to behold God's glory without the noise of external demands.

51

Such transformation is not instantaneous. Much like the gradual growth of a plant that needs consistent sunlight and water, spiritual growth in solitude requires consistent exposure to God's Word and prayer. Over time, believers may notice shifts in character, mindset, and priorities that reflect a deeper union with Christ. Former anxieties can give way to peace, anger can soften into compassion, and a desire to please people may diminish as the desire to please God intensifies.

3.3.2 Renewing the Mind and Heart

In times of intentional loneliness-turned-solitude, we open ourselves to divine instruction. Romans 12:2 exhorts us, "And do not be conformed to this world, but be transformed by the renewing of your mind." The world bombards us with messages that equate productivity with worth, busyness with importance, and social standing with identity. Solitude, however, allows us to disconnect from these cultural norms, focusing instead on God's perspective.

1. **Mind Renewal**: By meditating on Scripture and inviting the Holy Spirit to reorient our thinking, we begin to see ourselves, others, and the world through a kingdom lens. Negative self-talk yields to biblical truth—words of grace, purpose, and promise.

2. **Heart Renewal**: In solitude, unspoken emotions often surface. Feelings of hurt, anger, or shame come into the light of God's presence. Rather than suppressing or denying them, we can lift them to God, trusting His promise in **1 Peter 5:6–7** to humble ourselves under His mighty hand and cast all our cares upon Him. In His presence, our hearts can be purified, comforted, and restored.

3. **Will Alignment**: Another dimension of spiritual growth is the alignment of our will with God's. When Jesus prayed alone in Gethsemane (Matthew 26:36–44), He struggled with the cup of suffering He was about to endure. Yet through that solitary communion, He aligned His will with the Father's. Today, our smaller decisions—like how we spend our time, use our resources, or respond to difficult people—can also be surrendered in solitude. This daily practice of yielding fosters spiritual maturity.

3.3.3 The Role of Reflection and Examination

A practical way to facilitate spiritual growth in solitude is through reflection and self-examination, often aided by journaling. By writing down our prayers, insights, and even questions, we create a tangible record of our spiritual journey. This practice mirrors the biblical exhortation in Psalm 77:11–12, where the psalmist says, "I will remember the works of the LORD; surely I will remember Your wonders of old. I will also meditate on all Your work and talk of Your deeds." Journaling helps us "remember" what God has done, how He has answered prayers, and the ways He has shaped our character over time.

Such records become a reservoir of encouragement, especially when loneliness returns. Scanning previous entries can remind us of God's faithfulness in past seasons, reinforcing the conviction that He remains faithful now. Reflection also fosters an ongoing conversation with God, bridging the gap between our struggles and His power. Instead of isolating ourselves from issues, we invite the Holy Spirit into the center of them, trusting Him to illuminate areas needing repentance, healing, or growth.

3.4 Developing a Lifestyle of Seeking God Alone

3.4.1 Building Consistency in Quiet Pursuit

To truly transform loneliness into productive solitude, we must cultivate an ongoing practice of seeking God alone. Occasional retreats or sporadic moments of prayer can be refreshing, but they seldom produce long-lasting spiritual change if not woven into the fabric of daily life. The call to "seek His face continually" (1 Chronicles 16:11) underscores that this pursuit is meant to be habitual rather than episodic.

1. **Daily Appointments with God**: One simple yet powerful method is setting aside specific time slots each day for solitude. Whether it's early morning, midday, or late at night, having a consistent appointment with God underscores our commitment. In **Psalm 105:4**, we read, "Seek the LORD and His strength; seek His face evermore!" Marking a calendar or setting a phone reminder can transform these good intentions into an actionable plan.

2. **Weekly or Monthly Extended Times**: Beyond daily brief devotions, consider planning extended times of solitude. This might be a half-day retreat in nature, a quiet evening at home, or even a personal "mini-retreat" in a nearby location. These longer sessions allow for unhurried prayer, in-depth Scripture study, and reflective journaling.

3. **A Balanced Life**: Embracing a lifestyle of solitude does not mean neglecting the community. We still need fellowship, corporate worship, and shared ministry. Jesus Himself balanced solitude (Luke 6:12) with regular teaching,

healing, and fellowship with His disciples. The key lies in harmonizing alone time with active engagement, ensuring neither aspect is neglected.

3.4.2 Abiding in Christ: The Heart of Solitude

Ultimately, solitude is not an end in itself but a means to abide more fully in Christ. John 15:4 exhorts believers to "Abide in Me, and I in you. As the branch cannot bear fruit of itself... neither can you, unless you abide in Me." This abiding is an ongoing union, an active dependence on Jesus for every dimension of spiritual life. Solitude, then, becomes a natural extension of abiding—a regular withdrawal to reaffirm, refresh, and deepen our connection to the Vine.

During these times of private prayer, reflection, and worship, we reaffirm who Jesus is to us: Savior, Lord, Friend, and Shepherd. We acknowledge that all fruitfulness—be it in ministry, relationships, or personal character—flows from staying intimately connected to Him. Such abiding counters the world's frantic push for self-sufficiency, reminding us that we live and move and have our being in God (Acts 17:28).

3.4.3 Guarding the Heart and Mind in a Distracted Age

Modern culture bombards us with endless streams of entertainment, news, and social media updates. Even well-intentioned believers can find solitude elusive due to the persistent hum of notifications. Developing a lifestyle of seeking God alone necessitates intentional boundary-setting:

1. **Selective Media Consumption**: While not all digital content is harmful, unrestrained consumption can dull our spiritual

sensitivity. Choosing wisely what and how much we watch, read, or listen to safeguards our hearts. This discipline frees mental space for God's voice to be heard more clearly.

2. **Digital Sabbaths**: Consider designating certain hours or days as "tech-free." Turning off devices helps break the cycle of constant distraction, allowing room for deeper reflection and communion. **1 Thessalonians 5:17** reminds us to "pray without ceasing," a posture more feasible when we periodically disengage from digital noise.

3. **Sanctifying Our Thoughts**: Much of the battle for solitude occurs in our minds. In **Philippians 4:8**, Paul instructs us to dwell on whatever is "true, noble, just, pure, lovely, [and] of good report." By filtering our thoughts through this biblical lens, we foster an environment where solitude flourishes, even in day-to-day moments.

When we discipline ourselves to find consistent times of aloneness with God, we effectively transform a noisy life into one where moments of quiet intimacy become the norm. This lifestyle shift helps us maintain perspective, fostering a heart of worship and a willingness to hear God's whisper above the world's clamor.

3.5 Facing Challenges in Solitude

3.5.1 Confronting Spiritual Dryness and Distractions

Despite the many benefits of turning loneliness into solitude, believers often encounter challenges along the way. One common difficulty is spiritual dryness—a season where God's presence feels distant, and prayer seems fruitless. In Psalm 40:1, David testifies, "I waited patiently for the LORD; and He inclined to me, and heard my cry." Waiting implies that answers or consolations may not come immediately, even in solitude. These "dry" seasons test our perseverance and refine our faith, teaching us to trust God's timing rather than rely on emotional experiences.

Another stumbling block is distraction. Even if you carve out time to be alone with God, intrusive thoughts about to-do lists, unresolved conflicts, or personal worries can derail your focus. A practical response is to keep a notepad nearby to jot down tasks or concerns that arise; once noted, return your attention to God. This simple method helps you address recurring distractions without allowing them to dominate your solitude.

3.5.2 Battling Temptation and Negative Self-Talk

In solitude, unresolved temptations or negative self-talk can surface more acutely. Jesus Himself faced temptation during a period of solitude in the wilderness (Luke 4:1–13). Yet by relying on Scripture, He resisted the devil's distortions of truth. For us, Epheslans 6:10–11 Is a reminder to "be strong in the Lord and in the power of His might," putting on the armor of God so that we can stand against spiritual opposition.

- **Arming with Scripture**: Memorizing and meditating on specific verses that combat your personal struggles is vital. For instance, if self-condemnation arises, reflect on Romans 8:1 ("There is therefore now no condemnation to those who are in Christ Jesus").

- **Praying for Deliverance**: In solitude, we are free to cry out for God's help without fear of embarrassment or judgment. A heartfelt plea to the Holy Spirit—"Lead me not into temptation, but deliver me from the evil one" (paraphrase of Matthew 6:13)—opens the door for divine intervention.

3.5.3 Dealing with Fear and Anxiety in the Quiet Place

Ironically, solitude can exacerbate fears if we are unaccustomed to facing our inner turmoil. Without the usual distractions of social interactions or entertainment, latent anxieties may feel magnified. Yet this confrontation can be profoundly liberating. Isaiah 43:2 promises, "When you pass through the waters, I will be with you; and through the rivers, they shall not overflow you..." Though the context speaks to Israel's deliverance, the principle remains: God's companionship does not evaporate in times of fear.

- **Inviting God into Fear**: Instead of avoiding the anxious thoughts that arise, actively present them to God. Confess them, name them, and surrender them. Ask for His peace that surpasses understanding (Philippians 4:7).

- **Seeking Wise Counsel**: If anxiety becomes overwhelming, consider seeking counsel from a trusted pastor, Christian counselor, or spiritually mature friend. Solitude does not mean isolation from the resources God places in our lives.

- **Worship as Warfare**: Worship is a powerful tool against fear. Singing or playing worship music during solitude shifts focus from internal anxieties to God's sovereignty. This shift often ushers in a sense of calm and assurance.

Concluding Remarks

When approached through the lens of faith, loneliness can become a stepping stone rather than a stumbling block, directing our attention to the One whose comfort surpasses any human companionship. Rather than running from our sense of isolation, we can step into solitude deliberately, trusting that God will meet us there with grace, wisdom, and sustaining love. Whether you are brand-new to the discipline of solitude or have practiced it for years, the journey is ongoing—an ever-deepening invitation to meet the Lord in the secret place, where loneliness fades and eternal fellowship takes root.

If you found this message encouraging, please share it with others who may benefit. God Bless.

Chapter 4: Turning Your Solitude into God's Kingdom

Solitude is often viewed as a personal, individual practice—a time set aside for quiet reflection, prayer, or rest. Throughout this book, we have seen how seeking God in the secret place can transform our inner lives, grounding us in His love and dispelling the pangs of loneliness. Yet solitude carries an even broader purpose than merely enriching our own spiritual walk. In God's grand design, the personal renewal, insight, and strength we gain from time alone with Him are never meant to remain tucked away in isolation. Instead, they are vital resources for contributing to the flourishing of the body of Christ and the extension of God's kingdom on earth.

This chapter focuses on how our private moments of communion with the Lord not only shape us personally but also equip us for outward impact. We will see how solitude can sharpen spiritual gifts, align our hearts with God's mission, and empower us to serve others effectively. By exploring biblical examples, practical steps, and key scriptural principles, we will discover how to turn solitary encounters into kingdom-building momentum. When solitude propels us outward—toward the community of believers and the world at large—we begin to reflect Jesus, who frequently withdrew to lonely places and then emerged with renewed power and clarity for the work of God's kingdom.

4.1 The Purpose of Solitude in God's Kingdom

4.1.1 Understanding the Kingdom Context

When we talk about "God's kingdom," we refer to His sovereign rule, His righteous reign, and His redemptive plan actively unfolding in human hearts and societies. Jesus spoke repeatedly about the kingdom of heaven (or kingdom of God), describing it as both a present reality—accessible to those who believe—and a future culmination when God's reign will be fully realized at Christ's return (cf. Matthew 13:31–33, Luke 17:20–21). This kingdom is not limited by geography or political boundaries; it transcends earthly structures and is manifested wherever hearts submit to God's authority and reflect His righteousness, peace, and joy (Romans 14:17).

In Scripture, the call to participate in God's kingdom is both communal and individual. On the one hand, believers collectively form the church, entrusted with proclaiming God's message of salvation to the world (Matthew 28:19–20). On the other, each Christian has a personal responsibility to grow in Christlikeness,

61

exercise spiritual gifts, and contribute meaningfully to the body of Christ. Solitude—far from being a solitary pursuit with no wider implications—feeds directly into kingdom work by aligning our inner life with God's purposes. When we emerge from our times of private devotion, we do so ready to serve, lead, encourage, teach, and bring hope to others.

4.1.2 Linking Solitude to Mission

Although "mission" often conjures images of traveling to foreign lands or engaging in large-scale ministry, every believer partakes in God's mission simply by living out the gospel in daily life. Whether we are students, professionals, parents, or retirees, each of us holds the potential to influence our sphere for Christ. Solitude acts as a training ground, where we receive instruction, vision, and strength from the Holy Spirit to be effective witnesses of God's grace.

1. **Receiving Divine Direction:** In the Old Testament, we find a vivid example of how solitude precedes mission. After the prophet Elijah's dramatic victory on Mount Carmel (1 Kings 18), he fled into the wilderness, discouraged and fearful (1 Kings 19:1–4). It was there, in a solitary cave, that God spoke to him not through thunderous phenomena, but through a gentle whisper (1 Kings 19:12–13). God's instructions from that quiet encounter led Elijah to continue his prophetic ministry and anoint future leaders (1 Kings 19:15–18). This pattern—divine direction received in solitude—remains common today. In the silence, our ears become more attuned to God's voice, helping us discern His call for our lives.

2. **Refining Motives and Character:** Scripture places significant emphasis on the integrity and purity of those who serve in God's kingdom. For instance, in 2 Timothy 2:20–21, Paul uses the image of a great house containing vessels of different materials, urging believers to cleanse themselves so they can be vessels "for honor, sanctified and useful for the Master." Solitude provides a crucible where selfish ambition, pride, and impure motives can be exposed and surrendered to the Lord. If left unchecked, these hidden attitudes can undermine ministry, hinder relationships, and distort the gospel's portrayal in our lives.

3. **Cultivating Compassion for Others:** One of the paradoxes of solitude is that withdrawing from people can, paradoxically, heighten our empathy for them. In solitude, the Holy Spirit often stirs our hearts to pray for the needs of our family, church, and society with a deeper sense of urgency. This intercession shapes us into more compassionate believers who are ready to serve selflessly. The outward focus that emerges after solitude contrasts with self-centered withdrawal: rather than escaping from people permanently, we step back temporarily so that we can reengage with renewed tenderness and power.

Thus, solitude and kingdom mission are deeply intertwined. The personal transformation we experience alone with God naturally extends outward, becoming a blessing to others and a tangible representation of God's rule in the world.

4.2 Using Solitude to Develop Spiritual Gifts

4.2.1 Identifying and Understanding Spiritual Gifts

The New Testament teaches that every believer is endowed with one or more spiritual gifts—divine empowerments for serving the church and glorifying God. Passages like 1 Corinthians 12:7–11 and Romans 12:4–8 list gifts such as prophecy, teaching, service, exhortation, giving, leading, mercy, wisdom, healing, and the discernment of spirits, among others. The variety of gifts underscores the unity-in-diversity principle that characterizes the body of Christ. While we share a common faith, we function differently, each contributing uniquely to the kingdom's growth.

However, discovering one's spiritual gifts can be a challenging process, often complicated by societal pressures, self-doubt, or the fear of stepping into new areas of service. This is where solitude proves invaluable. By setting aside time to reflect, pray, and listen to the Holy Spirit, we create space to explore how God has uniquely wired us to serve. Psalm 139:13–14 reminds us that we are "fearfully and wonderfully made," highlighting God's intentional design in our lives. This design extends to our spiritual gifts, which align with His plan for our role in the church.

1. **Self-Examination Before God:** Solitude allows for a kind of spiritual inventory. We can ask ourselves: "Which activities for God's kingdom bring me a sense of deep joy and fulfillment? What do other believers affirm in my life as areas of gifting? In what contexts do I feel God's presence working powerfully through me?" Prayerfully presenting these questions to God in the quiet invites the Holy Spirit to guide our introspection, revealing dormant gifts or confirming those already recognized.

2. **Biblical Meditation:** Studying passages on spiritual gifts can trigger "aha" moments. For example, reading 1 Corinthians 12 with a humble, open heart in solitude can open our eyes

to gifts we have not yet considered. Sometimes, God may direct our attention to a particular verse or phrase that resonates with our experiences and passions. Journaling these insights helps ground them in Scripture rather than mere personal inclination.

3. **Listening for Divine Promptings:** Just as God spoke to biblical figures in silence, He can nudge our hearts about areas of service or deeper calling when we are still before Him. These promptings may come as a persistent idea, a mental picture, a scriptural phrase that surfaces repeatedly, or even a sense of peace about trying something new. Learning to distinguish God's gentle urgings from our own anxieties or assumptions is a skill honed in solitude, where external noise fades away.

4.2.2 Refining and Training Spiritual Gifts in the Quiet Place

Once we begin to identify our spiritual gifts, solitude becomes a workshop where God hones them further. Like any skill, spiritual gifts develop over time with practice and intentional cultivation, but the spiritual dimension requires dependence on the Holy Spirit rather than mere human effort.

1. **Prayerful Dedication of Gifts:** In solitude, we can consciously dedicate each gift back to God. For instance, if someone senses a gift of teaching, they might pray: "Lord, I offer my desire to teach Your Word. Sanctify this gift, guide me to learn sound doctrine, and grant me wisdom to present Your truth with clarity." Such prayers posture the heart in humility, acknowledging that our abilities are tools in God's hands rather than platforms for self-promotion.

2. **Studying Relevant Scriptures:** For any specific gift, the Bible contains insights on its proper use, potential pitfalls, and alignment with kingdom priorities. Someone sensing a gift of prophecy, for example, might study the lives of Old Testament prophets, gleaning lessons about boldness and integrity, while also examining New Testament directives about prophecy's role in edifying the church (1 Corinthians 14). Solitude provides ample opportunity to delve into these scriptural contexts, bridging historical understanding with present-day application.

3. **Seeking the Spirit's Empowerment:** Spiritual gifts are not natural talents that function on human ability alone. They require the Holy Spirit's enabling power (1 Corinthians 12:11). Through solitary prayer, believers can invite fresh infillings of the Spirit, acknowledging that any fruitfulness in ministry stems from God's gracious provision. This reliance on divine strength fuels perseverance, especially when challenges arise or when stepping out into new areas of service feels daunting.

4. **Personal Retreats for Depth:** While daily devotions are essential, periodic retreats focused on gift development can accelerate growth. During a weekend of solitude in a retreat center or a few dedicated hours at home, believers can plan extended times of prayer, reflection, and study specifically related to their gifts. This concentrated investment often yields breakthroughs—new insights, renewed passion, or confirmation of the Spirit's anointing.

4.2.3 Biblical Examples of Gifted Solitude

Numerous biblical figures experienced solitude as a crucible for honing their unique callings:

- **Moses and Leadership**: Before confronting Pharaoh and leading Israel, Moses spent years in Midian as a shepherd (Exodus 2:15–22; 3:1–2). This season of relative solitude refined his character and prepared him to shepherd an entire nation.

- **Nehemiah and Administration**: When Nehemiah heard of Jerusalem's broken walls, his initial response was prayerful mourning and fasting in solitude (Nehemiah 1:4). That private intercession birthed a strategic plan to rebuild the city, revealing his administrative gift empowered by divine guidance.

- **John the Baptist and Prophetic Boldness**: Scripture portrays John the Baptist as a voice "crying in the wilderness" (John 1:23). His isolated life in the desert was foundational to his bold, countercultural ministry, preparing Israel's hearts for the Messiah.

In each case, solitude was not an endpoint but a formative space. By engaging with God away from the demands of society, these individuals nurtured gifts essential to their mission, eventually emerging to fulfill pivotal roles in God's unfolding story.

4.3 Solitude as Preparation for Serving Others

4.3.1 Cultivating Compassion, Empathy, and Love

One might question how solitude, which removes us from the immediate presence of others, could possibly deepen our care for them. Yet Scripture points to love as the hallmark of genuine faith:

"By this all will know that you are My disciples, if you have love for one another" (John 13:35). Solitude can powerfully nurture this love by placing our hearts before God's transforming presence.

- **Encountering God's Heart**: In quiet reflection, the Holy Spirit often impresses upon us the depth of God's compassion. We recall verses like Psalm 145:9, which attests to God's "tender mercies over all His works," or Matthew 9:36, where Jesus is "moved with compassion" for the crowds. Immersing ourselves in such passages, we catch a glimpse of God's own empathy, fueling a desire to reflect that same love to those around us.

- **Repentance and Renewal**: Solitude also allows God to confront any selfishness, bitterness, or prejudice lurking in our hearts. By surrendering these attitudes, we make room for the Spirit to instill genuine compassion. The result is not a forced or superficial concern for others but a heartfelt empathy that mirrors Christ's love.

- **Intercession for People**: Another practical outworking of love in solitude is intercessory prayer. Lifting up specific individuals, communities, or global issues to God often enlarges our perspective. We begin to see people not as irritants or mere acquaintances but as souls precious to the Lord. That shift in vision can spark tangible acts of kindness once we step back into daily life.

4.3.2 Listening for God's Instructions on Whom to Serve

Often, the question isn't whether we should serve, but whom and how. With the myriad needs in the world, it's easy to become overwhelmed or paralyzed by indecision. Solitude offers the crucial

68

space for discerning God's leading:

1. **Personal Burdens as Clues:** In the hush of prayer, certain concerns may weigh heavily on our spirits. We might feel an unshakable burden for the homeless, for at-risk youth, for global missions, or for unchurched neighbors in our city. Rather than dismissing these burdens, we can view them as possible indicators of God's assignment.

2. **Biblical Guidance:** Studying passages about godly service can clarify our role. For instance, James 1:27 highlights caring for orphans and widows as a pure expression of faith. Micah 6:8 underscores doing justly, loving mercy, and walking humbly with God. While these verses apply broadly, the Spirit can illuminate specific ways to live them out, whether through local volunteering or global outreach.

3. **Holy Promptings:** Sometimes, in solitude, we sense a clear prompting—perhaps to reach out to a particular family, to volunteer in a church ministry, or to start a small Bible study. These directives may come as persistent ideas we can't shake or an unmistakable sense of peace about a certain course of action..

4.3.3 Distinguishing Self-Initiated Projects from God-Initiated Service

A crucial aspect of kingdom work is ensuring that our service stems from divine commission rather than merely personal ambition. While good intentions matter, not every project is God's best plan for us. In solitude, we learn to differentiate between impulses driven by ego—like seeking recognition or feeling pressured to prove our worth—and genuine callings that align with God's kingdom agenda.

- **Testing the Fruit:** Jesus taught that a tree is known by its fruit (Matthew 7:16–18). Likewise, God-inspired service tends to bear lasting, life-giving results. It builds up others, fosters unity, and directs glory back to God. By contrast, self-initiated endeavors can lead to burnout, strife, or frustration when we operate outside God's grace for a particular assignment.

- **Seeking Confirmation:** Once we sense an idea in solitude, it's wise to seek confirmation from Scripture, trusted mentors, or fellow believers who can pray alongside us. This communal discernment prevents us from running off on tangents or missing the counsel of wise voices. When a prompting is truly from God, He often provides multiple confirmations that resonate with biblical principles and the counsel of spiritually mature individuals.

By processing these questions in solitude, we prepare ourselves to serve not out of mere emotion but under the Spirit's guidance and empowerment. Ultimately, service that flows from solitude is anchored in the love and clarity we receive from God, making it both more sustainable and more fruitful in advancing His kingdom.

4.4 Turning Private Devotion into Public Impact

4.4.1 The Synergy Between Hidden Devotion and Public Ministry

A foundational biblical principle is that what happens in private often shapes the fruitfulness of public ministry. Jesus declared, "Your Father who sees in secret will reward you openly" (Matthew 6:6). While this verse addresses prayer specifically, the principle extends to other dimensions of devotion—like fasting, generosity, or solitude. Our quiet, uncelebrated acts of communion with God forge the spiritual backbone for any external work.

- **Integrity and Authenticity:** Public ministry without a private devotional life is hollow. Over time, it may devolve into performance or hypocrisy. When we consistently seek God in solitude, however, authenticity is nurtured. We preach or serve from a place of genuine conviction, having wrestled with truths in our own hearts before presenting them to others.

- **Resilience in Trials:** Public service invites challenges: criticism, opposition, fatigue, or even spiritual attack. The anchor that holds us steady is the reservoir of grace built up during solitude. Like an athlete who trains in private to build endurance for a race, a believer fortified in secret communion can endure public storms without losing heart.

- **Glorifying God, Not Self:** Genuine ministry aims to direct attention toward God. The humility fostered in solitude curtails our tendency to seek applause. When accolades do come, we are quicker to redirect them heavenward, recognizing that any anointing or skill is purely God's gift. This posture stands in stark contrast to the self-promotional culture of our age.

4.4.2 Overcoming the Fear of Public Engagement

For some, the transition from private devotion to public witness can be intimidating. Fear of judgment or failure might hold them back. Solitude, however, can serve as the training ground where we confront and surrender these fears:

1. **Gaining God's Perspective:** In prayerful solitude, we refocus on God's greatness and sufficiency. Verses like Deuteronomy 31:8 ("the Lord, He is the One who goes before you") reassure us that we do not step into ministry alone. When we see the size of God relative to our challenges, fear shrinks into perspective.

2. **Practicing Obedience in Small Steps:** Sometimes, the key to overcoming fear is incremental obedience. Rather than waiting for a grand, stage-like ministry, we can start by sharing our testimony with one friend, leading a small Bible discussion group, or volunteering in a modest capacity at church. Each small act of faith expands our confidence for future tasks.

3. **Receiving the Spirit's Power:** The Holy Spirit equips us for boldness. In Acts 4:31, early believers prayed together and "were all filled with the Holy Spirit, and they spoke the word of God with boldness." Though the context involved collective prayer, personal solitude equally can be a moment of Spirit-filled empowerment. Inviting the Holy Spirit to embolden our witness transforms timidity into courage.

4.4.3 Stories of Personal Transformation and Community Influence

History abounds with believers whose private devotion led to notable public impact:

- **Susanna Wesley:** Known as the "Mother of Methodism," Susanna Wesley raised John and Charles Wesley, whose ministries shaped Christian history. Despite a busy household, she carved out private prayer time daily by pulling her apron over her head. This unwavering commitment to solitude and prayer profoundly influenced her children, who led spiritual revivals across England and beyond.

- **William Carey**: Called the "father of modern missions," William Carey was a humble cobbler who spent countless hours in solitary study of Scripture and geography. His quiet devotion birthed a vision to take the gospel to India, sparking the modern missions movement.

- **Gladys Aylward**: A British missionary to China, Gladys Aylward was initially rejected by mission boards. Yet her solitary times with God anchored her conviction to go. Despite numerous hardships—political upheaval, poverty, and cultural barriers—her personal faith and prayer life fueled her to rescue orphans and evangelize effectively.

In each case, private devotion was the seed from which public influence grew. These stories illustrate the kingdom principle: solitude is not an end unto itself but a wellspring that empowers believers to shape their families, neighborhoods, and entire nations for Christ.

4.5 Living a Balanced Life: Solitude and Community

4.5.1 The Tension Between Retreat and Engagement

Christians often oscillate between craving times of withdrawal to recharge spiritually and recognizing their duty to remain present in community. An overemphasis on solitude can lead to isolation and neglect of fellowship; an overemphasis on communal activity can crowd out the quiet spaces needed for deep personal growth.

Achieving a healthy balance is key to sustaining spiritual vitality and missional effectiveness.

- **Biblical Mandate for Community:** The New Testament underscores believers' interconnectedness: "Now you are the body of Christ, and members individually" (1 Corinthians 12:27). We need each other's gifts, encouragement, and even correction. Without community, we risk stagnation and limited perspective.

- **Balancing Personal and Corporate Worship:** Acts 2:46–47 depicts the early church gathering regularly in the temple courts (corporate worship) and breaking bread from house to house (smaller fellowship). These communal expressions did not negate personal devotion; rather, they complemented it. Solitude refuels us for meaningful corporate worship, and fellowship refines us by placing us in relationships where love must be practiced tangibly.

4.5.2 Jesus as the Supreme Model

Throughout the Gospels, Jesus models this tension perfectly. He frequently withdrew to pray alone (Luke 5:16), yet His public ministry was highly relational—teaching crowds, mentoring disciples, eating in people's homes, and welcoming children. His rhythm of engagement and retreat stands as a blueprint:

1. **Morning Prayer and Daily Ministry:** Mark 1:35–38 captures a typical pattern in Jesus' life: rising early to pray in a solitary place, followed by preaching in local towns. The solitary prayer cultivated intimacy with His Father, from which flowed power and direction for ministering to the masses.

2. **Periodically Escaping the Crowds:** Before critical junctures—like selecting the Twelve or heading toward the crucifixion—Jesus took extended retreats. For instance, Luke 6:12–13 describes Him spending a whole night in prayer prior to choosing the apostles. By anchoring pivotal decisions in solitude, He demonstrated reliance on the Father's guidance rather than crowd pressures or even the disciples' opinions.

3. **Maintaining Compassionate Engagement:** Even as He sought solitude, Jesus never dismissed genuine human need. In Matthew 14:13–14, upon hearing of John the Baptist's death, Jesus tried to withdraw privately, but the crowds followed Him. Instead of turning them away, He "was moved with compassion" and healed their sick. This shows that solitude can coexist with a responsive heart toward urgent needs.

By following Jesus' example, we learn to hold solitude and community in proper tension. A life that neglects either is incomplete, missing out on either the rejuvenation of personal communion or the growth and joy found in Christ-centered relationships.

4.5.3 Accountability, Encouragement, and Shared Purpose

Balancing solitude and community also involves practical considerations for accountability and encouragement:

- **Partnering in Prayer:** While solitude is personal, sharing prayer requests with trusted friends or a small group can lead to powerful intercession that accelerates spiritual breakthroughs. We see glimpses of corporate prayer

75

throughout Acts, where believers prayed with one accord for boldness, guidance, and miraculous intervention (Acts 4:23–31). Solitude does not exclude such communal dynamics; instead, it enriches them as each believer brings fresh insight gleaned from alone time with God.

- **Mentoring and Discipleship:** Spiritual mentors or discipleship relationships can help us process insights gained in solitude. A mentor might challenge us to act on convictions formed in private prayer, ensuring that we don't stay in the realm of lofty ideals without practical application. Likewise, we can become mentors ourselves, using what God imparts in the quiet place to guide newer believers.

- **Pursuing a Shared Mission:** The body of Christ is diverse, with myriad callings that intersect to form a collective mission. Solitude equips us for our specific calling, while community ensures these callings are woven into a unified tapestry that glorifies God. Ephesians 4:16 emphasizes how each part of the body works together, increasing the church's overall maturity and ability to impact the world.

Hence, a robust, kingdom-focused life hinges on weaving solitude and fellowship seamlessly. Neither realm fully substitutes for the other; rather, they operate in synergy, each amplifying the richness and effectiveness of the other.

Concluding Remarks

As you meditate on this chapter, consider practical ways you might steward your solitary moments for the greater good. Ask God to reveal how He wants to use your unique gifts, passions, and experiences to extend His kingdom among your friends, workplace, church, and broader society. Reflect on the balance you hold between private devotion and public engagement—have you leaned too heavily on one side? How might you recalibrate to mirror the balanced rhythm Christ modeled?

In embracing solitude not as an isolated pursuit but as a gateway to kingdom impact, we participate in the divine pattern exemplified by saints and servants of God across centuries. Indeed, the stillness of the prayer closet is the place where giants of faith are formed, where heavenly assignments are birthed, and where hearts are kindled with the compassion that propels them into a hurting world. May our solitary encounters with the Father continually inform and inspire us to be agents of His redemptive reign, shining as lights in the darkness, proclaiming in word and deed that the kingdom of God has come near.

If you found this message encouraging, please share it with others who may benefit. God Bless.

Chapter 5: People Been in Solitude— From the Bible

Throughout the Scriptures, we encounter individuals whose solitary experiences shaped not only their personal faith but also the trajectory of God's redemptive work in history. Unlike modern assumptions that solitude is purely an introspective or lonely endeavor, these biblical accounts reveal that time spent alone with God often yields transformative outcomes—for the individual and for entire communities. In this final chapter, we examine five major figures who entered periods of solitude under varying circumstances and for different divine purposes: Moses, Elijah, David, Jesus, and Paul.

Each of their stories highlights a distinct dimension of biblical solitude: from receiving divine instruction and revelation to overcoming despair, from preparing for leadership to interceding for others, and from confronting personal weaknesses to ultimately influencing nations. Their examples remind us that solitude is not merely a backdrop for spiritual reflection but a sacred stage where God's power, comfort, and guidance manifest in unparalleled ways.

As you read this chapter, let the lives of these solitary figures inspire you to see how personal encounters with God can become catalysts for communal blessing, how moments of isolation can birth unimaginable breakthroughs, and how every believer, regardless of era or context, can find deep purpose and intimacy in the quiet places of fellowship with the Almighty.

5.1 Moses: Solitude on the Mountain

Moses' story is marked by a recurring theme of encountering God in solitary spaces—from a lonely desert at the burning bush to the lofty heights of Mount Sinai. If there is a biblical figure who demonstrates how solitude can radically alter both personal destiny and an entire nation's trajectory, it is Moses. Though he was raised in Egyptian royalty, his defining moments often occurred far from palaces and crowds.

5.1.1 Meeting God in Isolation

The Book of Exodus famously begins with Moses' dramatic origin story. Born at a perilous time for Israelite infants, he was preserved by divine providence, and then brought up in Pharaoh's palace. Yet, as a young adult, Moses fled Egypt after intervening in the harsh treatment of a Hebrew slave. This flight led him into the Midianite wilderness—a stark, solitary environment that set the stage for a life-changing encounter with God.

The Burning Bush Experience

- **Location of Divine Encounter**: Moses was tending sheep near Mount Horeb (also referred to as the "Mountain of God") when he noticed a bush engulfed in flames yet not consumed (Exodus 3:1-6) This paradoxical sight compelled him to investigate.

- **God's Self-Revelation**: In that quiet, unpopulated space, God called Moses by name. The Lord introduced Himself as the God of Abraham, Isaac, and Jacob, establishing continuity with the patriarchs who had come before.

- **Solitude as Spiritual Threshold**: Moses found himself on "holy ground," and asked to remove his sandals—a symbolic act of reverence. The solitude of this desert location removed distractions, making Moses acutely aware of God's holiness and his own unworthiness.

Here, we see a microcosm of how isolation can become sacred territory where God's presence is tangibly experienced. Had Moses stayed amid the bustle of Egypt's courts or even the busyness of Midian's settlements, he might have missed this revelatory moment. The desert environment, though outwardly desolate, was internally rich with the possibility of divine communion.

God's Commission

- **A Reluctant Prophet**: Moses' initial reaction to God's call was reluctance. He questioned his own capabilities ("Who am I that I should go to Pharaoh?") and even asked God to send someone else (Exodus 4:13). Solitude thus exposed Moses' insecurities. However, it also became the setting where God addressed his fears directly.

- **Empowering the Weak**: The Lord promised Moses that He would be with him, providing Aaron as a spokesman, and equipping him with signs to convince Pharaoh. In this solitary exchange, Moses transitioned from a fugitive shepherd to the chosen liberator of an enslaved nation.

Moses' desert solitude illustrates a fundamental biblical principle: God often reveals Himself and entrusts significant callings to people in quiet, out-of-the-way settings. In these places of isolation, human limitations are confronted, and divine empowerment becomes the solution. The pattern remains true today: when we feel inadequate or afraid, the solitude we seek with God can become a womb for unimaginable spiritual birth, fueling us for tasks that seem far beyond our natural capacity.

5.1.2 The Role of Solitude in Receiving God's Law

While Moses' encounter at the burning bush was a pivotal awakening, his most famous experience of solitude came later, at Mount Sinai, after the Israelites had miraculously escaped Egypt. Through the parted waters of the Red Sea, they journeyed to the foot of this imposing mountain, where the next phase of Moses' solitary communion with God would have ramifications for all of Israel—and indeed, for religious communities across millennia.

Ascending Mount Sinai

- **An Invitation to Meet God**: In Exodus 19, the Lord invited Moses to ascend the mountain, promising to speak with him there. No one else—neither priests nor the general Israelite population—was permitted to approach. This exclusive invitation underscores the holiness of God and the solemnity of the message He intended to deliver.

- **Extended Periods of Separation**: Moses spent forty days and nights on Sinai (Exodus 24:18), immersed in an encounter with God that was both terrifying (the mountain trembled, enveloped in smoke and lightning) and awe-inspiring. This extended solitude was not a spiritual luxury; it was an appointment where Moses listened intently and received precise instructions.

Receiving the Ten Commandments

- **Moral and Ethical Cornerstone**: The Ten Commandments, etched by the finger of God onto tablets of stone, formed the covenantal bedrock of Israel's relationship with the Almighty. Delivered in that isolated mountain setting, these commandments outlined how the people were to worship God and conduct themselves in society.

- **Deeper Revelations of Law and Worship**: Beyond the Ten Commandments, Moses received detailed instructions about tabernacle construction, priestly garments, sacrificial offerings, and social justice. The solitude of the mountain allowed for comprehensive revelation, unbroken by human opinions or daily disruptions.

- **Community Transformation from Solitary Encounters**: When Moses returned from the mountain, his face shone with God's glory (Exodus 34:29). This radiance symbolized not only the lingering effect of divine presence but also served as evidence that solitude can tangibly alter a person—spiritually, emotionally, and even physically. Through Moses' solitary experiences, an entire nation received God's moral framework and learned the importance of worshiping the Lord in both ritual and lifestyle.

Intercession and Spiritual Leadership

- **A Mediator in Solitude**: On more than one occasion, Moses used his solitary access to God to intercede for the Israelites. When they sinned by worshiping the golden calf (Exodus 32), Moses returned to the mountain, pleading with God not to destroy them. The fervency of his solitary prayer averted divine wrath.

- **Bearing the People's Burdens**: These episodes highlight how individual solitude can serve a communal purpose. Moses was not seeking time alone for personal tranquility; he was fulfilling a mediatorial role, bridging the gap between a holy God and a wayward people.

By observing Moses' pattern of ascent to and descent from the mountain, we see how solitude was integral to receiving guidance that would shape the moral fabric of a nation. Today, believers might not trek up a literal mountain to hear from God, yet the principle remains: dedicated time alone with the Lord can yield insights, convictions, and wisdom that bless not only ourselves but also those whom we serve or influence. Moses stands as a testament that in the hush of solitude, we can receive revelations capable of transforming entire communities.

5.2 Elijah: Solitude in the Wilderness

The prophet Elijah emerges in the biblical narrative during a tumultuous period of Israel's history. Righteous kings were scarce, rampant idolatry plagued the land, and spiritual compromise was widespread. Elijah's prophetic ministry was bold, dramatic, and fraught with danger—enough to make him one of the most memorable figures in the Old Testament. Yet, he found strength, clarity, and a renewed mission in solitude.

5.2.1 Finding Strength in Isolation

Elijah's call to prophesy against corrupt rulers like King Ahab and Queen Jezebel required both courage and conviction. At times, this calling forced him into hiding, underscoring the life-or-death stakes of his ministry.

Fleeing to the Brook Cherith

- **Divine Instruction to Hide**: After Elijah foretold a devastating drought in Israel (1 Kings 17:1), God directed him to go eastward and hide by the Brook Cherith. This remote stream, unknown to the rest of the populace, became Elijah's refuge.

- **Provision in the Wilderness**: At Cherith, Elijah experienced daily miracles of provision: ravens brought him bread and meat, and the brook provided water (1 Kings 17:4-6). This miraculous sustenance underscores that solitude, though physically isolating, can be a place where God's care is astonishingly evident.

Dependence and Spiritual Formation

- **Learning God's Faithfulness**: Cherith symbolized a divine training ground. Cut off from human society, Elijah learned absolute reliance on God. Without the familiarity of communal life, he witnessed God's unerring faithfulness in new, intimate ways.

- **Emotional and Mental Fortitude**: Being alone in the wilderness likely tested Elijah's endurance. The prophet would have confronted fear, loneliness, and uncertainty, yet each meal provided by the ravens reinforced that the One who called him was also sustaining him. This refining process solidified Elijah's inner strength, preparing him for dramatic confrontations yet to come—particularly on Mount Carmel.

5.2.2 How God Speaks in the Stillness

The narrative of Elijah reaches a climactic point in 1 Kings 18 with the famous showdown on Mount Carmel, where he challenged the prophets of Baal, and God sent fire from heaven to validate Elijah's message. However, this triumphant moment was followed by a severe personal crisis. Threatened by Jezebel, Elijah fled once more—this time deeper into the wilderness.

Despair and Divine Encounter at Horeb

- **The Prophet's Burnout**: In 1 Kings 19, Elijah, overwhelmed and fearful, asked God to take his life. It is a jolting contrast: the same man who fearlessly confronted idol-worshipers felt utterly undone soon after. Emotional exhaustion often follows intense spiritual victories, pointing to the delicate balance between public ministry and personal resilience.

- **Angel's Ministry and Forty-Day Journey**: As Elijah lay despondent, an angel appeared, providing food and urging him to journey to Mount Horeb. This second mountain (also known as Sinai) was a sacred place, deeply connected to Israel's history. Elijah traveled forty days and nights, mirroring Moses' period of solitude.

- **A "Still, Small Voice"**: Once on Horeb, Elijah encountered a series of dramatic phenomena: wind strong enough to tear rocks apart, a powerful earthquake, and consuming fire (1 Kings 19:11-12). Yet God was not in these grand displays. Rather, He spoke to Elijah in a "still, small voice" or a gentle whisper. This moment is often cited as a prime biblical illustration that God's presence is not always accompanied by spectacle; He also meets us in quiet subtlety.

Renewed Commission in Solitude

- **God's Reassurance**: Confronting Elijah's despair and sense of isolation, God reassured him that he was not alone—that 7,000 faithful remained in Israel (1 Kings 19:18). In solitude, Elijah gained a more accurate perspective.

- **Next Steps Revealed**: Far from allowing Elijah to remain in desolation, God laid out specific instructions—anointing future kings and identifying Elisha as the prophet's successor (1 Kings 19:15-16). This re-commissioning showed that Elijah's time alone was not an end but a prelude to further service.

From Elijah's experiences, we glean two vital lessons. First, solitude can be an arena where we confront the depths of our discouragement and discover that God meets us in our rawest moments. Second, God often communicates not in thunderous drama but in gentle whispers—nudging our hearts into a stillness we can only find when we withdraw from the clamor of everyday life. Elijah's wilderness sojourns thus highlight how solitude can replenish the prophet's heart, revive a sense of divine call, and offer clarity that bustling environments rarely afford.

5.3 David: Solitude as a Shepherd and a King

King David is a multifaceted figure in the biblical narrative—shepherd, musician, warrior, poet, fugitive, and eventually the ruler of Israel. While his life is filled with public exploits—defeating Goliath, uniting the tribes, and establishing Jerusalem as the capital—his journey is also punctuated by significant periods of solitude. These solitary experiences became the wellspring of many psalms that continue to inspire believers worldwide.

5.3.1 Worshiping Alone with God

David's path to kingship did not begin in the grandeur of a palace but in the fields of Bethlehem, tending his father Jesse's sheep. Long before the prophet Samuel anointed him as the future king, David's heart was shaped in the quiet expanses of pastureland.

Shepherding and Hymns of Praise

- **Time for Reflection**: Shepherds in ancient Israel spent long hours watching over their flocks, often in relative isolation. In David's case, these hours provided ample opportunity to observe nature, practice his skill with the harp, and direct his thoughts toward God.

- **Psalms of Devotion**: Many biblical scholars surmise that David composed some of his early psalms during these pastoral days. The recurring imagery of God as a shepherd (Psalm 23) or as a majestic creator (Psalm 8) likely sprang from David's solitary meditations under star-filled skies and wide-open fields.

- **Developing Musical and Spiritual Gifts**: Solitude allowed David to hone both his musical ability and his worshipful spirit. Far from being a mundane chore, shepherding became a training ground where David cultivated a profound awareness of God's presence.

Inner Formation Before Outer Conquest

- **Facing Challenges**: Even as a youth, David confronted threats—lions and bears that endangered the flock (1 Samuel 17:34-37). In solitude, he learned courage and reliance on God, lessons that would later apply to more imposing giants on the battlefield.

- **Readiness to Serve**: By the time David encountered Goliath, he was already armed with a rich history of trusting God in hidden moments. The self-assurance he displayed in front of Israel's army was not pride; it was the outgrowth of countless hours spent alone, placing his life and his flock in God's hands.

David's early days reveal how private worship fosters inner strength. While others might have viewed shepherding as a lonely and lowly job, David discovered that God was intimately near in the fields. His heart became so attuned to the Lord that he spontaneously erupted into praise, penning words that still resonate today. In David's solitude, we see the birth of a worshiper—one whose private devotion paved the way for extraordinary public exploits.

5.3.2 How Solitude Prepared Him for Leadership

David's trajectory from shepherd to king did not progress in a straight line. Animosity from King Saul forced David into extended periods of fugitive life in wilderness strongholds, caves, and foreign territories. Ironically, these harrowing episodes of isolation further refined him for the throne.

Caves of Adullam and En-Gedi

- **Fleeing Saul**: Jealous of David's military successes and his rising popularity, Saul sought to kill him. Consequently, David and his loyal supporters fled into remote areas (1 Samuel 22-24). For a season, David's "court" consisted of men described as distressed, indebted, and discontented—a far cry from the prestige of a palace.

- **Learning Patience and Mercy**: On at least two occasions, David had the chance to kill Saul and claim the throne but chose restraint (1 Samuel 24 and 26). Solitude taught David to trust God's timing rather than hasten his rise to power through violence. This restraint demonstrated extraordinary maturity and godliness—fruits of a heart molded by time alone in prayer and reflection.

Refining Character in Adversity

- **Dependence on God**: The psalms composed during David's fugitive years often depict a man wrestling with fear yet clinging to divine promises. Psalm 57, for instance, bears the inscription "when he fled from Saul in the cave," underscoring how these solitary hideouts became sanctuaries of worship.

- **Leading in the Shadows**: David's leadership skills were honed in makeshift communities of outcasts, forging loyalty and camaraderie in dire conditions. Through these experiences, he gained empathy for the marginalized—a trait that would mark his reign with compassion.

When David finally ascended to the throne, his extended solitude shaped him into a leader with profound spiritual depth. He was neither a naive shepherd boy nor a battle-hardened tyrant, but a man after God's own heart (1 Samuel 13:14). His solitary years had taught him humility, reliance on divine providence, and a spirit of worship that permeated his rule. Even in later life, when he made grave mistakes, David's reflex was to repent before God (see Psalm 51), an attitude cultivated over countless solitary hours of personal communion.

Thus, David's story highlights how solitude lays the foundation for wise and compassionate leadership. While few of us will rule a nation, each of us may find ourselves entrusted with responsibilities—whether in family, work, or ministry contexts. David shows that the deeper our private fellowship with God, the more authentic and impactful our public leadership can be.

5.4 Jesus: Seeking Solitude with the Father

No figure exemplifies the transformative power of solitude more profoundly than Jesus. Though fully divine, He lived a fully human life, demonstrating that intimacy with the Father is neither optional nor secondary but integral to fulfilling one's purpose. The Gospels are replete with moments when Jesus intentionally withdrew from the crowds, revealing that even the busiest of ministries requires sacred pauses for renewal and guidance.

5.4.1 The Example of Christ's Retreats

Jesus ministered in a context of high demand: people flocked to Him for healings, exorcisms, and teachings. His disciples needed constant mentoring, and critics perpetually sought ways to discredit Him. Despite these pressures, Jesus consistently carved out space for solitude.

Early Morning Prayer

- **Mark 1:35** records that Jesus rose "very early in the morning, while it was still dark," departing to a solitary place to pray. The day before had been packed with miracles and crowds. Yet, instead of indulging in extra sleep, Jesus prioritized communion with His Father.

- **Modeling Dependence**: By seeking solitude at the start of the day, Jesus showcased absolute dependence on the Father's will. This private time was not an add-on but the source of His authority and clarity for each day's ministry.

Departing to Desolate Places

- **Regular Pattern**: Luke 5:16 notes that Jesus "would withdraw to desolate places and pray." The original Greek suggests an ongoing habit, indicating that retreat was woven into His routine, not just reserved for crisis moments.

- **Biblical Theology of Rest**: Jesus' example highlights a broader biblical theology of rest, resonating with God's command for the Sabbath. Even the Messiah, who carried the world's weight, took breaks from active service, illustrating that we, too, need recurrent intervals of spiritual replenishment.

5.4.2 How Jesus Used Solitude Before Major Events

Crucially, Jesus' solitude often preceded or followed pivotal moments, suggesting that such retreats fortified Him for critical tasks and decisions.

Preparation for Public Ministry

- **Forty Days in the Wilderness**: Before launching His public ministry, Jesus spent forty days in the Judean wilderness, fasting and enduring satanic temptations (Matthew 4:1-11; Luke 4:1-13). In this time of utter isolation, He confronted the devil's cunning offers—provision, protection, and power. Each temptation targeted a different facet of Jesus' identity and mission.

- **Victory Through the Word**: In responding with Scripture, Jesus demonstrated that time spent alone with God had ingrained in Him a profound grasp of His Father's Word and will. Emerging triumphant from these temptations, He commenced a ministry marked by unwavering obedience to the Father.

Choosing the Twelve Disciples

- **A Momentous Decision**: Luke 6:12-13 describes Jesus spending an entire night in prayer before selecting His twelve apostles. This decision would shape the future of the church, as these men would carry the gospel to the far corners of the earth after Jesus' ascension.

- **Guidance Through Extended Prayer**: The fact that Jesus prayed through the night underscores the gravity of the choice at hand. His example implies that when believers face life-altering decisions—be they personal or ministry-related—solitary prayer can yield clarity that might be missed in hurried petitions.

Solitude After Intense Ministry

- **Post-Feeding the Five Thousand**: After miraculously feeding a vast crowd, Jesus sent His disciples ahead by boat and dismissed the multitudes (Matthew 14:22-23). Then, He ascended a mountain by Himself to pray. This pattern of withdrawal after high-intensity ministry speaks volumes about self-care and spiritual recalibration.

- **Regaining Perspective**: By slipping away, Jesus modeled how external success—like feeding thousands—must not distract from the primary relationship with the Father. No matter how impactful His public work, He returned repeatedly to the wellspring of solitude to remain spiritually centered.

Gethsemane's Solitary Agony

- **The Ultimate Reckoning**: On the night before His crucifixion, Jesus prayed alone in the Garden of Gethsemane. While He brought Peter, James, and John for moral support, He ultimately moved "a little farther" to wrestle alone with the impending agony (Matthew 26:36-39).

- **Surrendering to the Father's Will**: It was in this wrenching solitude that Jesus uttered, "Not as I will, but as You will," modeling complete surrender. Even the best-intentioned disciples failed to stay awake, underscoring that certain spiritual battles can only be fought in isolation with God.

Jesus' solitary practices emphasize that communion with God is not reserved for special occasions or crisis points alone; rather, it is the consistent undercurrent that sustains a life of obedience. If the Son of God found it necessary to retreat, how much more should we, finite and frail as we are, take deliberate steps to be alone with our Maker? Christ's example is a beacon showing that solitude leads to alignment with the Father's will, strength against temptation,

93

discernment for major decisions, and comfort in the darkest hours.

5.5 Paul: From Isolation to Influence

The Apostle Paul's life is among the most radical transformations depicted in the New Testament. A zealous persecutor of Christians turned into the most prolific missionary of the early church, Paul penned epistles that continue to shape Christian theology and discipleship. Yet behind his public ministry lies a lesser-known chapter of solitude that set the foundation for his far-reaching influence.

5.5.1 How Solitude Transformed His Ministry

Paul's conversion on the road to Damascus is often recounted for its dramatic imagery: a blinding light, the voice of Jesus, and a humbled Paul (then known as Saul) led by the hand into the city (Acts 9:1-9). What followed, however, was not an immediate plunge into missionary endeavors but a season of solitude and reflection.

Retreat to Arabia

- **Galatians 1:15-18**: In his letter to the Galatians, Paul reveals that soon after his conversion, he "went away into Arabia" for an unspecified duration before returning to Damascus. This detail is not elaborated upon in the Acts narrative, leaving some aspects to scholarly inference.

- **Purpose of Withdrawal**: Scholars suggest that Paul used this time to reconcile his Pharisaic training with his newfound faith in Christ. Having encountered the risen Jesus, the core of his theological framework needed re-examination. This solitary period likely involved deep study of Hebrew Scriptures, prayer, and an internalization of the gospel message he once opposed.

Emerging with a Christ-Centered Theology

- **Revelation Independent of Apostles**: Paul emphasizes that his gospel did not come from human sources but through the revelation of Jesus Christ (Galatians 1:11-12). Solitude in Arabia could have been the crucible where this revelation was clarified, forming the bedrock of Paul's future teachings on justification by faith and the believer's union with Christ.

- **Intimacy with the Risen Lord**: The abrupt shift from persecutor to proponent likely stirred questions and possibly loneliness, as the Christian community initially feared him. Yet in that isolated interval, Paul built a relationship with the Lord that transcended his past. The once-violent zealot became a man consumed by love for Christ.

5.5.2 The Connection Between Time with God and Bold Evangelism

Upon returning from Arabia and spending some time in Damascus, Paul began an active ministry that would span decades, crossing cultural and geographical boundaries. His epistles frequently reference hardships—imprisonments, beatings, and shipwrecks—yet also showcase an unwavering passion for the gospel. The seeds of this fervor and resilience can be traced, in part, to his solitary experiences.

Foundational Doctrinal Clarity

- **Romans, Galatians, Ephesians**: Paul's letters delve into profound theological truths—election, grace, the nature of the church, spiritual gifts, and more. This doctrinal depth suggests a significant period of personal meditation and wrestling with Scripture. In solitude, he grasped truths that would later revolutionize the early church's understanding of salvation and mission.

- **Boldness Beyond Human Approval**: Paul's readiness to confront religious authorities and to plant churches in hostile territories indicates a faith anchored in divine calling rather than human endorsement. He often faced criticism—even from fellow believers concerned about Gentile inclusion—but stood firm on revelations received in private communion with God.

Unwavering Confidence in Christ

- **Suffering and Comfort**: Passages like 2 Corinthians 1:3-11 reveal Paul's perspective on suffering: that it unites believers to Christ's afflictions and fosters reliance on God. The capacity to interpret suffering in redemptive terms was likely shaped by solitary reflection, where Paul poured out his pain and received divine consolation.

- **Prayerful Dependence**: Time and again, Paul asks churches to pray for him—that he might speak the gospel boldly (Ephesians 6:19). Despite his formidable intellect and tenacity, he recognized that effective ministry hinged on spiritual empowerment. Solitude had taught him that abiding in Christ was not a cliché but a prerequisite for any authentic kingdom work.

Mentoring and Writing Ministries

- **Discipling Younger Leaders**: Paul's encouragement of Timothy, Titus, and others reveals a man intent on passing the torch of faith. The pastoral letters brim with guidance on church order, character development, and perseverance. These insights, so essential for nurturing fledgling communities, flow from the deep well Paul developed in private communion with God.

- **Epistles from Prison**: Some of Paul's most treasured letters—Ephesians, Philippians, Colossians, and Philemon—were written under house arrest or in prison. These enforced isolations echoed earlier seasons of solitude, compelling Paul to write letters that have instructed believers for centuries. His physical confinement did not stifle his spiritual influence; if anything, it heightened it.

Paul's narrative testifies that solitude can be the crucible where theological convictions solidify, spiritual dependence deepens, and boldness for evangelism emerges. While his missionary journeys and public preaching garnered widespread attention, the hidden chapters of isolation and reflection underpinned his enduring legacy. Modern believers may not replicate Paul's itinerant lifestyle, but we can learn that behind every sustained work for the kingdom lies a private devotion—often cultivated in stillness—that grants resilience, clarity, and an unwavering sense of divine commissioning.

Concluding Remarks

As you reflect on these lives, consider how your own seasons of solitude—even when prompted by unwelcome circumstances— might be precisely where God intends to reveal Himself more fully.

The Bible's witness is clear: solitude is far from mere isolation. It can serve as a corridor to divine revelation, a sanctuary for authentic worship, an antechamber for kingdom assignments, and a workshop for crafting the character necessary to fulfill those assignments.

- **Embrace the Desert Places**: If you find yourself in a wilderness—literal or metaphorical—remain open to the possibility that God is uniquely present there. Rather than viewing solitude as a curse, see it as an invitation to deeper fellowship.

- **Seek Revelation and Transformation**: Follow the example of these biblical figures by actively listening, praying, and surrendering your fears and ambitions. Allow solitude to be a space for personal introspection and realignment with God's purposes.

- **From Solitude to Service**: Remember that biblical solitude never terminates in self-absorption. Moses descended to Sinai with laws to guide Israel, Elijah resumed his prophetic mission, David rejoined community life as king, Jesus returned to minister to the masses, and Paul traveled extensively to plant churches. Solitude is always a springboard, sending us back into relationships and responsibilities with renewed clarity and love.

In witnessing how Moses, Elijah, David, Jesus, and Paul encountered God in solitary realms, we catch a glimpse of the vast potential that lies within our own lonely seasons. Their stories encourage us not to flee from quietness or lament isolation as purely negative, but to step into those times with expectancy. There, in silence, God can meet us, shape us, and equip us for roles we never imagined. Indeed, if biblical history is any guide, some of the most pivotal works of grace and redemption often begin in places far removed from the public eye, but intimately close to the heart of God.

If you found this message encouraging, please share it with others who may benefit. God Bless.

www.ingramcontent.com/pod-product-compliance
Lightning Source LLC
Chambersburg PA
CBHW071502070426

42452CB00041B/2112